Pennsylvania
Real Estate Practice Exams
for 2015-2016

by

Jim Bainbridge, J.D.

© 2015

City Breeze Publishing LLC
P.O. Box 12650
Marina del Rey, California 90250

ISBN: 978-1-939526-24-3

PRINTED IN THE UNITED STATES OF AMERICA

About the Author

Jim Bainbridge is a graduate of Harvard Law School and has been an active member of the California Bar for more than 30 years. He is a licensed California real estate broker, and a past recipient of a National Science Foundation Fellowship for graduate studies in mathematics at UC Berkeley. He is the author of *PSI Real Estate Exam Prep 2015-2016*, *California Real Estate Principles and License Preparation*, and numerous works that have been published in more than 50 journals in the USA, UK, Canada, Australia, Japan, and the Netherlands.

Mr. Bainbridge is also a member of the Real Estate Educators Association (REEA) and has been recognized as a Certified Distance Education Instructor by IDECC, which is a function of the Association of Real Estate License Law Officials.

DISCLAIMER and LIMIT of LIABILITY

Introduction

Thank you for purchasing *Pennsylvania Real Estate Practice Exams for 2015-2016*. This book is intended to help you prepare for — and pass — both the state and the national portion of the Pennsylvania Real Estate exam. This book consists of:

- four 110-multiple-choice-question practice exams — 30 state-portion questions and 80 national-portion questions on each exam;

- detailed answers given for all of the questions, allowing you to assess your strengths and weaknesses — and to hone your test-taking skills — before exam day;

- a comprehensive review of the real estate math that you are expected to know for the Pennsylvania exam;

- a useful glossary of over 600 key real estate terms for test preparation and reference, and;

- tips on preparing for and taking the Pennsylvania exam.

Of course, this book of practice exams is no substitute for a study of the real estate principles contained in pre-licensing courses. Before you take these practice exams, you should have a thorough knowledge of these real estate principles. If you do not, you may become discouraged by your scores on these practice exams — and confidence will serve you well on your quest to pass the Pennsylvania exam and become a real estate licensee.

A thorough, up-to-date review of the real estate principles covered in the national portion of the Pennsylvania real estate exam is provided in the supplemental textbook, *PSI Real Estate Prep 2015-2016*, written by Jim Bainbridge, the author of the following practice exams.

Table of Contents

EXAM TEST-TAKING TIPS..**6**

DEFINITIONS OF KEY REAL ESTATE TERMS..**8**

REAL ESTATE MATH...**43**

Section 1: Basic Math Concepts 43

Section 2: Calculations for Transactions, Including Mortgage Calculations........................... 46

Section 3: Property Tax Calculations 46

Section 4: Prorations (utilities, rent, property taxes, insurance, etc.)................................. 47

Section 5: Calculations for Valuation... 52

PRACTICE EXAM #1: **55**

ANSWERS TO PRACTICE EXAM #1:..**77**

PRACTICE EXAM #2: **84**

ANSWERS TO PRACTICE EXAM #2:..**106**

PRACTICE EXAM #3: **114**

ANSWERS TO PRACTICE EXAM #3:..**136**

PRACTICE EXAM #4: **144**

ANSWERS TO PRACTICE EXAM #4:..**166**

EXAM TEST-TAKING TIPS

- The Pennsylvania real estate exam potentially covers a vast amount of real estate knowledge; therefore, taking practice exams — and studying the answers that you get wrong — during the weeks immediately prior to exam day can be highly beneficial.

- You will be graded on the number of correct answers you give. You will not be penalized for giving incorrect answers. Therefore, it is important to answer all of the questions, even if you are not sure of the correct answer. Often, of the four possible answers presented, at least two answers are clearly wrong. Of the remaining two, both might appear correct, in which case you should choose the answer that you feel is the better one. If you cannot decide which one is the better, take your best guess — you'll probably have about a 50-50 chance of being correct.

- Take the time to read each question carefully. It is altogether too easy to interpret a question in a way that you expect the question to read, rather than as it is actually stated. This is especially true for questions that are stated in the negative ("it is not true that..." or "which of the following is false"). Other keywords that can significantly alter the meaning of a question are "except," "but," "if," and "generally."

- Do not rush to choose an answer just because you are relatively certain that it is true. This is because there may be two or more answers given that correctly answer the question, in which case such answers as "both a and b" or "all of the above" may be the best, and correct, answer.

- If math is your most problematic and anxiety producing area, consider saving the math questions to the end and coming back to them when you have completed the rest of the exam. This will prevent you from becoming frustrated and discouraged through most of the exam and will likely give you more time to figure out the correct answers to the math questions.

- You should try to estimate the correct answer to math questions before you begin your calculations. If you find that your estimate is far different from the result of your calculation, carefully go back and check your calculation. Also, be aware that the possible answers presented for math questions usually contain answers that examinees can arrive at by making some common error, such as by calculating based on the number of years rather than on the number of months. Therefore, just because the result of your calculation exactly matches one of the possible answers does not mean that your result is correct.

- Additionally, math real estate questions often use "none of the above" as the fourth possible answer. This means that if you do not get an answer that matches one of the first three possible answers, either your calculation was incorrect or the correct exam answer is "none of the above."

- Because the extensive glossary included in this book includes terms often found on Pennsylvania real estate exams, it is recommended that you review these important key real estate terms at least once each week prior to taking the official Pennsylvania exam.

- Finally, if you complete the exam early, as many examinees do, take the remaining time to read over as many of the questions as you can to be sure that you did not make the all-too-common mistake of misreading certain questions the first time around. As you take the following practice exam, you will probably find that you make several "foolish" errors — errors that result not from your lack of knowledge, but from your failure to carefully read certain questions that can at times appear to be a bit tricky. Don't let such "foolish" errors spoil the result of your official exam.

Good luck! And may you have a long and rewarding career as a real estate licensee.

DEFINITIONS OF KEY REAL ESTATE TERMS

1031 exchange — under Internal Revenue Code section 1031, a tax-deferred exchange of "like kind" properties.

1099-S Reporting — a report to be submitted on IRS Form 1099-S by escrow agents to report the sale of real estate, giving the seller's name, Social Security number, and the gross sale proceeds.

abendum clause — a clause in a deed, usually following the granting clause and beginning with the words "to have and to hold," that describes the type of estate being transferred.

acknowledgment — a written declaration signed by a person before a duly authorized officer, usually a notary public, acknowledging that the signing is voluntary.

acknowledgment of satisfaction — a written declaration signed by a person before a duly authorized officer, usually a notary public, acknowledging that a lien has been paid off in full and that the signing is voluntary.

abandonment — failure to occupy or use property that may result in the extinguishment of a right or interest in the property.

abatement — a legal action to remove a nuisance.

abstract of judgment — a summary of the essential provisions of a court monetary judgment that can be recorded in the county recorder's office of the county or counties in which the judgment debtor owns property to create a judgment lien against such properties.

abstract of title — a chronological summary of all grants, liens, wills, judicial proceedings, and other records that affect the property's title.

abstractor — the person who prepares an abstract of title.

acceleration clause — a clause in either a promissory note, a security instrument, or both that states that upon default the lender has the option of declaring the entire balance of outstanding principal and interest due and payable immediately.

acceptance — consent (by an offeree) to an offer made (by an offeror) to enter into and be bound by a contract.

accession — the acquisition of additional property by the natural processes of accretion, reliction, or avulsion, or by the human processes of the addition of fixtures or improvements made in error.

accretion — a natural process by which the owner of riparian or littoral property acquires additional land by the gradual accumulation of soil through the action of water.

accrued depreciation — depreciation that has happened prior to the date of valuation.

acknowledgment — a written declaration signed by a person before a duly authorized officer, usually a notary public, acknowledging that the signing is voluntary.

acknowledgment of satisfaction — a written declaration signed by a person before a duly authorized officer, usually a notary public, acknowledging that a lien has been paid off in full and that the signing is voluntary.

active investor — an investor who actively contributes to the management of the business invested in.

actual agency — an agency in which the agent is employed by the principal, either by express agreement, ratification, or implication.

ad valorem — a Latin phrase meaning "according to value." The term is usually used regarding property taxation.

adjustable-rate mortgage (ARM) — a mortgage under which interest rates applicable to the loan vary over the term of the loan.

adjusted cost basis — the dollar amount assigned to a property after additions of improvements and deductions for depreciation and losses are made to the property's acquisition cost.

adjustment period — the time intervals in an adjustable-rate mortgage during which interest rates are not adjusted.

administrator — a person appointed by a probate court to conduct the affairs and distribute the assets of a decedent's estate when there was no executor named in the will or there was no will.

advance fee — a fee charged in advance of services rendered.

adverse possession — the process by which unauthorized possession and use of another's property can ripen into ownership of that other's property without compensation.

after-acquired interests — all interests in a property acquired subsequent to a transfer of the property.

affirmative covenant — a contractual promise to do certain acts, such as to maintain a party wall, the remedy for breach thereof being either monetary damages or injunctive relief, not forfeiture.

age-life method — *see*, straight-line method.

agency — the representation of a principal by an agent.

agent — a person who represents another.

alienation clause — a due-on-sale clause

alluvium — addition to land acquired by the gradual accumulation of soil through the action of water.

ambulatory instrument — a document that can be changed or revoked, such as a will.

amended public report — a report that a subdivider must apply for if, after the issuance of a final public report, new conditions arise that affect the value of the subdivision parcels.

Americans with Disabilities Act — a federal act that prohibits discrimination against persons with disabilities, where "disability" is defined as "a physical or mental impairment that substantially limits a major life activity."

amortization — in general, the process of decreasing or recovering an amount over a period of time; as applied to real estate loans, the process of reducing the loan principal over the life of the loan.

anchor bolt — a bolt inserted into concrete that secures structural members to the foundation.

annual percentage rate (APR) — expresses the effective annual rate of the cost of borrowing, which includes all finance charges, such as interest, prepaid finance charges, prepaid interest, and service fees.

appraisal — an estimate of the value of property resulting from an analysis and evaluation made by an appraiser of facts and data regarding the property.

appreciation — an increase in value due to any cause.

appropriation, right of — the legal right to take possession of and use for beneficial purposes water from streams or other bodies of water.

appurtenance — an object, right or interest that is incidental to the land and goes with or pertains to the land.

asbestos — a naturally occurring mineral composite that once was used extensively as insulation in residential and commercial buildings, in brake pads, and in fire-retardant products, such as furniture. As asbestos ages, it breaks down to small fibers that, if inhaled in sufficient quantity over sufficient time, can cause a variety of ailments, including a type of cancer known as mesothelioma.

assignment — the transfer of the rights and obligations of one party (the assignor) to a contract to another party (the assignee); a transfer of a tenant's entire interest in the tenant's leased premises.

associate broker — a person with a real estate brokers license who is employed as a salesperson by another broker.

assumption — an adoption of an obligation that primarily rests upon another person, such as when a purchaser agrees to be primarily liable on a loan taken out by the seller.

attachment lien — a prejudgment lien on property, obtained to ensure the availability of funds to pay a judgment if the plaintiff prevails.

attorney in fact — a holder of a power of attorney.

automatic homestead —a homestead exemption that applies automatically to a homeowner's principal residence and that provides limited protection for the homeowner's equity in that residence against a judgment lien foreclosure.

average price per square foot — the average price per square foot for a given set of properties is arrived at by adding the per-square-foot cost of each property in the set by the number of properties in the set.

avulsion — a process that occurs when a river or stream suddenly carries away a part of a bank and deposits it downstream, either on the same or opposite bank.

back-end ratio — the ratio of total monthly expenses, including housing expenses and long-term monthly debt payments, to monthly gross income.

balloon payment — a payment, usually the final payment, of an installment loan that is significantly greater than prior payments — "significantly greater" generally being considered as being more than twice the lowest installment payment paid over the loan term.

bankruptcy — a legal process conducted in a United States Bankruptcy court, in which a person declares his or her inability to pay debts.

beam — a horizontal member of a building attached to framing, rafters, etc., that transversely supports a load.

bearing wall — a wall that supports structures (such as the roof or upper floors) above it. In condominiums, non-bearing walls are owned by the individual condominium owners, whereas bearing walls usually are property owned in common.

beneficiary — (1) the lender under a deed of trust, (2) one entitled to receive property under a will, (3) one for whom a trust is created.

bequeath — to transfer personal property by a will.

bequest — a gift of personal property by will.

bilateral contract — a contract in which a promise given by one party is exchanged for a promise given by the other party.

bill of sale — a written document given by a seller to a purchaser of personal property.

blanket mortgage — a mortgage used to finance two or more parcels of real estate.

blight — as used in real estate, the decline of a property or neighborhood as a result of adverse land use, destructive economic forces, failure to maintain the quality of older structures, failure to maintain foreclosed homes, etc.

blind ad — an advertisement that does not disclose the identity of the agent submitting the advertisement for publication.

blockbusting — the illegal practice of representing that prices will decline, or crime increase, or other negative effects will occur because of the entrance of minorities into particular areas.

board foot — a unit of measure of the volume of lumber, equivalent to the volume of lumber of 1 square foot and 1 inch thick; 144 cubic inches.

bona fide — in good faith; authentic; sincere; without intent to deceive.

book depreciation — a mathematical calculation used by tax authorities and accountants to determine a depreciation deduction from gross income.

book sale — a "sale" for accounting purposes regarding tax-delinquent property; this "sale" does not entail an actual transfer property.

boot — cash or other not like-kind property received in an exchange.

bridge loan — a short-term loan (often referred to as a swing loan) that is used by a borrower until permanent financing becomes available.

broker — a person who, for a compensation or an expectation of compensation, represents another in the transfer of an interest in real property.

brownfields — as defined by the EPA, "real property, the expansion, redevelopment, or reuse of which may be complicated by the presence or potential presence of a hazardous substance, polluted, or contaminant."

BTU (British Thermal Unit) — A measure of heating (or cooling) capacity equivalent to the amount of heat required to raise the temperature of 1 pound of water 1° Fahrenheit (from 39°F to 40°F).

buffer zone — in zoning, a strip of land to separate, or to ease the transition from, one use to another, such as a park separating a residential zone from a commercial zone, or a commercial or industrial zone separating residential zones from busy streets or highways.

bulk sale — a sale, not in the ordinary course of the seller's business, of more than half of the value of the seller's inventory as of the date of the bulk sale agreement.

bundle of rights — rights the law attributes to ownership of property.

business opportunity — involves the sale or lease of the assets of an existing business enterprise or opportunity, including the goodwill of the business or opportunity, enabling the purchaser or lessee to begin a business.

buyer's agent — a real estate broker appointed by a buyer to find property for the buyer.

capital asset — permanent, non-inventory assets held for personal or investment purposes, such as householders' homes, household furnishings, stocks, bonds, land, buildings, and machinery.

capital gain — the amount by which the net sale proceeds from the sale of a capital asset exceeds the adjusted cost value of the asset.

capitalization approach — *see*, income approach

capitalization rate — the annual net income of a property divided by the initial investment in, or value of, the property; the rate that an appraiser estimates is the yield rate expected by investors from comparable properties in current market conditions.

capture, law of — the legal right of a landowner to all of the gas, oil, and steam produced from wells drilled directly underneath on his or her property, even if the gas, oil, or steam migrates from below a neighbor's property.

carryover —under an adjustable-rate loan, an increase in the interest rate not imposed because of an interest-rate cap that is carried over to later rate adjustments.

caulking — a putty-like material used to seal cracks and joints to make tight against leakage of air or water, as in making windows watertight.

CC&Rs — an abbreviation of "covenants, conditions, and restrictions" — often used to refer to restrictions recorded by a developer on an entire subdivision.

certificate of occupancy — a written document issued by a local governmental agency, stating that a structure intended for occupancy has been completed, inspected, and found to be habitable.

chain of title — a complete chronological history of all of the documents affecting title to the property.

chattel real — personal property that contains some interest in real property, the most common example being a lease.

Civil Rights Act of 1866 — a federal law enacted during Reconstruction that stated that people of any race may enjoy the right to enforce contracts, to sue, be parties, and give evidence, to inherit, purchase, lease, sell, hold, and convey real and personal property, and to full and equal benefit of all laws.

Civil Rights Act of 1968 — a federal law (often referred to as the Fair Housing Act) that prohibited discrimination in housing based on race, creed, or national origin. An amendment to this Act in 1974 added prohibition against discrimination based on gender, and an amendment in 1988 added prohibition against discrimination based on a person's disabilities or familial status.

client — an agent's principal

closing — in reference to an escrow, a process leading up to, and concluding with, a buyer's receiving the deed to the property and the seller's receiving the purchase money.

cloud on title — any document, claim, lien, or other encumbrance that may impair the title to real property or cast doubt on the validity of the title.

coastal zone — a region where significant interaction of land and sea processes occurs.

Coastal Zone Management Act (CZMA) — a federal act intended to protect coastal zones, including the fish and wildlife that inhabit those zones, of the Atlantic, Pacific, and Arctic oceans, the Gulf of Mexico, Long Island Sound, and the Great Lakes from harmful effects due to residential, commercial, and industrial development.

collar beam — a beam connecting pairs of opposite rafters well above the attic floor.

column — a circular or rectangular vertical structural member that supports the weight of the structure above it.

commercial acre — the buildable part of an acre that remains after subtracting land needed for streets, sidewalks, and curbs.

commingling — regarding trust fund accounts, the act of improperly segregating the funds belonging to the agent from the funds received and held on behalf of another; the mixing of separate and community property.

commission — an agent's compensation for performance of his or her duties as an agent; in real estate, it is usually a percent of the selling price of the property or, in the case of leases, of rentals.

common interest development (CID) — a subdivision in which purchasers own or lease a separate lot, unit, or interest, and have an undivided interest or membership in a portion of the common area of the subdivision.

community apartment project — a development in which an undivided interest in the land is coupled with the right of exclusive occupancy of an apartment located thereon.

community property — property owned jointly by a married couple or by registered domestic partners, as distinguished from separate property. As a general rule, property acquired by a spouse or registered domestic partner through his/her skills or personal efforts is community property.

community property with right of survivorship — property that is community property and that has a right of survivorship. Upon the death of a spouse or registered domestic partner, community property with right of survivorship passes to the surviving spouse or domestic partner without probate.

comparable property — a property similar to the subject property being appraised that recently sold at arm's length, where neither the buyer nor the seller was acting under significant financial pressure.

comparative market analysis (CMA) — a comparison analysis made by real estate brokers using recent sales, and current listings, of similar nearby homes to determine the list price for a subject property.

competitive market analysis (CMA) — *see*, comparative market analysis.

compound interest — the type of interest that is generated when accumulated interest is reinvested to generate interest earnings from previous interest earnings.

concealment — the act of preventing disclosure of something.

condemnation proceeding — a judicial or administrative proceeding to exercise power of eminent domain.

condition subsequent — a condition written into the deed of a fee estate that, if violated, may "defeat" the estate and lead to its loss and reversion to the grantor.

conditional use — a zoning exception for special uses such as churches, schools, and hospitals that wish to locate to areas zoned exclusively for residential use.

condominium — a residential unit owned in severalty, the boundaries of which are usually walls, floors, and ceilings, and an undivided interest in portions of the real property, such as halls, elevators, and recreational facilities.

conduit — a (usually) metal pipe in which electrical wiring is installed.

conflict of interest — a situation in which an individual or organization is involved in several *potentially* competing interests, creating a risk that one interest *might* unduly influence another interest.

conforming loan — a loan in conformance with FHFA guidelines.

consideration — anything of value given or promised, such as money, property, services, or a forbearance, to induce another to enter into a contract.

conspiracy — in antitrust law, occurs when two or more persons agree to act and the agreed-upon action has the effect of restraining trade.

construction mortgage — a security instrument used to secure a short-term loan to finance improvements to a property.

constructive eviction — a breach by the landlord of the covenant of habitability or quiet enjoyment.

constructive notice — (1) notice provided by public records; (2) notice of information provided by law to a person who, by exercising reasonable diligence, could have discovered the information.

contingency — an event that may, but is not certain to, happen, the occurrence upon which the happening of another event is dependent.

contract — a contract is an agreement to do or to forbear from doing a certain thing.

conventional loan — a mortgage loan that is not FHA insured or VA guaranteed.

conversion — the unauthorized misappropriation and use of another's funds or other property.

cooperating broker — a broker who attempts to find a buyer for a property listed by another broker.

co-ownership — joint ownership

cost approach — an appraisal approach that obtains the market value of the subject property by adding the value of the land (unimproved) of the subject property to the depreciated value of the cost (if currently purchased new) of the improvements on subject property.

cost recovery — the recoupment of the purchase price of a property through book depreciation; the tax concept of depreciation.

cost-to-cure method — a method of calculating depreciation by estimating the cost of curing the curable depreciation and adding it to the value of the incurable depreciation.

counteroffer — a new offer by an offeree that acts as a rejection of an offer by an offeror.

coupled with an interest — an aspect of an agency that refers to the agent's having a financial interest in the subject of the agency, which has the legal effect of making the appointment of the agent irrevocable.

covenant — a contractual promise to do or not do certain acts, such as on a property, the remedy for breach thereof being either monetary damages or injunctive relief, not forfeiture.

crawlspace — the space between the ground and the first floor that permits access beneath the building.

credit bid — a bid at a foreclosure sale made by the beneficiary up to the amount owed to the beneficiary.

credits — in reference to an escrow account, items payable to a party. This definition of a debit does not conform to its use in double-entry bookkeeping or accounting.

cubic-foot method — a method of estimating the replacement or reproduction cost of a structure that is similar to the square-foot method except that it uses the volume of recently constructed similar buildings. This method often is used for warehouses and other industrial buildings

curable depreciation — depreciation that results from physical deterioration or functional obsolescence that can be repaired or replaced at a cost that is less than or equal to the value added to the property.

debits — in reference to an escrow account, items payable by a party. This definition of a debit does not conform to its use in double-entry bookkeeping or accounting.

deed — a document that when signed by the grantor and legally delivered to the grantee conveys title to real property.

deed in lieu of foreclosure — a method of avoiding foreclosure by conveying to a lender title to a property lieu of the lender's foreclosing on the property.

defeasance clause — a provision in a loan that states that when the loan debt has been fully paid, the lender must release the property from the lien so that legal title free from the lien will be owned by the borrower.

defendant — the one against whom a lawsuit is brought.

deferred maintenance — any type of depreciation that has not been corrected by diligent maintenance.

deficiency judgment — a judgment given to a lender in an amount equal to the balance of the loan minus the net proceeds the lender receives after a judicial foreclosure.

deliberate misrepresentation — *see*, intentional misrepresentation

designated agent — an agent authorized by a real estate broker to represent a specific principal to the exclusion of all other agents in the brokerage. This designated agent owes fiduciary responsibilities to the specified principal, but other agents in the brokerage may represent other parties to the same transaction that the specified principal is a party to without creating a dual agency situation. Where this practice of designated agency is allowed, disclosure of the designated agency relationship is required.

demand — the level of desire for a product.

Depository Institutions Deregulation and Monetary Control Act (DIDMC) — a federal law that exempts from state usury laws interest paid on residential mortgage loans.

deposit receipt — a written document indicating that a good-faith deposit has been received as part of an offer to purchase real property; also called a purchase and sale agreement.

depreciation — the loss in value due to any cause.

depreciation deduction — an annual tax allowance for the depreciation of property.

devise — (1) (noun) a gift of real property by will; (2) (verb) to transfer real property by a will.

devisee — a recipient of real property through a will.

discounted rate — a rate (also called a teaser rate) on an adjustable-rate mortgage that is less than the fully indexed rate.

discount points — a form of prepaid interest on a mortgage, or a fee paid to a lender to cover cost the making of a loan. The fee for one discount point is equal to 1% of the loan amount.

disintegration — the phase when a property's usefulness is in decline and constant upkeep is necessary.

divided agency — an agency in which the agent represents both the seller and the buyer without obtaining the consent of both.

documentary transfer tax — a tax imposed by counties and cities on the transfer of real property within their jurisdictions.

dominant tenement — land that is benefited by an easement appurtenant.

dormer — a projecting structure built out from a sloping roof that is used to provide windows and additional headroom for the upper floor.

down payment — the amount of money that a lender requires a purchaser to pay toward the purchase price.

drywall — prefabricated sheets or panels nailed to studs to form an interior wall or partition.

dual agent — a real estate broker who represents both the seller and the buyer in a real estate transaction.

due diligence — the exercise of an honest and reasonable degree of care in performing one's duties or obligations. A real estate agent's due diligence involves investigating the property to ensure that the property is as represented by the seller and to disclose accurate and complete information regarding the property.

due-on-sale clause — a clause in the promissory note, the security instrument, or both that states that the lender has the right to accelerate the loan if the secured property is sold or some other interest in the property is transferred.

duress — unlawful force or confinement used to compel a person to enter into a contract against his or her will.

earnest money deposit — a deposit that accompanies an offer by a buyer and is generally held in the broker's trust account.

easement — a non-possessory right to use a portion of another property owner's land for a specific purpose, as for a right-of-way, without paying rent or being considered a trespasser.

easement appurtenant — an easement that benefits, and is appurtenant to, another's land.

easement by necessity —arises as a creation of a court of law in certain cases were justice so demands, as in the case where a buyer of a parcel of land discovers that the land he or she just purchased has no access except over the land of someone other than from the person from whom the parcel was purchased.

easement in gross — an easement that benefits a legal person rather than other land.

eaves — the overhang of a roof that projects over an exterior wall of a house.

economic life — the period of time that the property is useful or profitable to the average owner or investor.

economic obsolescence — *see*, external obsolescence.

EER and SEER — Air-conditioners have an efficiency rating that states the ratio of the cooling capacity (how many BTUs per hour) to the power drawn (in watts). For room air conditioners the ratio is the EER (energy efficiency ratio); for central air conditioners the rating is the SEER (seasonal energy efficiency ratio). The higher the EER or SEER, the greater the efficiency of the air-conditioning unit. Significant savings in electricity costs can be obtained by installing more efficient air-conditioning units.

effective age — the age of an improvement that is indicated by the condition of the improvement, as distinct from its chronological age.

effective demand — demand coupled with purchasing power sufficient to acquire the property from a willing seller in a free market.

effective gross income — income from a property after an allowance for vacancies and uncollectible rents is deducted from gross income.

ejectment — a legal action to recover possession of real property from a person who is not legally entitled to possess it, such as to remove an encroachment or to evict a defaulting buyer or tenant.

emancipated minor — a minor who, because of marriage, military service, or court order, is allowed to contract for the sale or purchase of real property.

emblements — growing crops, such as grapes, avocados, and apples, that are produced seasonally through a tenant farmer's labor and industry.

eminent domain — right of the state to take, through due process proceedings (often referred to as condemnation proceedings), private property for public use upon payment of just compensation.

employee — a person who works for another who directs and controls the services rendered by the person.

employer — a person who directs and controls the services rendered by an employee.

encroachment — a thing affixed under, on, or above the land of another without permission.

encumber — To place a lien or other encumbrance on property.

encumbrance — A right or interest held by someone other than the owner the property that affects or limits the ownership of the property, such as liens, easements, licenses, and encroachments.

Endangered Species Act — a federal law that is intended to provide a means whereby the ecosystems upon which endangered species and threatened species depend may be conserved, and to provide a program for the conservation of such endangered species and threatened species.

Environmental Impact Statement (EIS) —) a written document that federal agencies must prepare for any development project that a federal agency could prohibit or regulate, and any development project for which any portion is federally financed. An EIS can include comments on the expected impact of a proposed development on such things as air quality, noise, population density, energy consumption, water use, wildlife, public health and safety, and vegetation.

Equal Credit Opportunity Act (ECOA) — a federal law that prohibits a lender from discriminating against any applicant for credit on the basis of race, color, religion, national origin, sex, marital status, or age (unless a minor), or on the grounds that some of the applicant's income derives from a public assistance program.

equal dignities rule — a principle of agency law that requires the same formality to create the agency as is required for the act(s) the agent is hired to perform.

equilibrium — the period of stability when the property changes very little.

equitable title — the right to possess and enjoy a property while the property is being paid for.

escalator clause — a provision in a lease that provides for periodic increases in rent in an amount based on some objective criteria not in control of either the tenant or the landlord, such as the Consumer Price Index.

escheat — a process whereby property passes to the state if the owner of the property dies intestate without heirs, or if the property becomes abandoned.

escrow — a neutral depository in which something of value is held by an impartial third party (called the escrow agent) until all conditions specified in the escrow instructions have been fully performed.

escrow agent — an impartial agent who holds possession of written instruments and deposits until all of the conditions of escrow have been fully performed.

escrow holder — an escrow agent

escrow instructions — the written instructions signed by all of the principals to the escrow (buyers, sellers, and lenders) that specify all of the conditions that must be met before the escrow agent may release whatever was deposited into escrow to the rightful parties.

estate — the degree, quantity, nature, duration, or extent of interest one has in real property.

estate at sufferance — a leasehold that arises when a lessee who legally obtained possession of a property remains on the property after the termination of the lease without the owner's consent. Such a holdover tenant can be evicted like a trespasser, but if the owner accepts rent, the estate automatically becomes a periodic tenancy.

estate at will — an estate (or tenancy) in which a person occupies a property with the permission of the owner; however, the tenancy has no specified duration, and, in most states, may be terminated at any time by either the tenant or the owner of the property upon giving proper notice.

estate for years — a leasehold that continues for a definite fixed period of time, measured in days, months, or years.

estate from period to period — a leasehold that continues from period to period, whether by days, months, or years, until terminated by proper notice.

estate of inheritance — a freehold estate.

estoppel — a legal principle that bars one from alleging or denying a fact because of one's own previous actions or words to the contrary. Ostensible agency can be created by estoppel when a principal and an unauthorized agent act in a manner toward a third-party that leads the third party to rely on the actions of the unauthorized agent, believing that the actions are authorized by the principal.

exclusive agency listing — a listing agreement that gives a broker the right to sell property and receive compensation (usually a commission) if the property is sold by anyone other than the owner of the property during the term of the listing.

exclusive authorization and right to sell listing — a listing agreement that gives a broker the exclusive right to sell property and receive compensation (usually a commission) if the property is sold by anyone, including the owner of the property, during the term of the listing.

executed contract— a contract that has been fully performed; may also refer to a contract that has been signed by all of the parties to the contract.

executor — a person named in a will to carry out the directions contained in the will.

executory contract — a contract that has not yet been fully performed by one or both parties.

express contract — a contract stated in words, written or oral.

external obsolescence — depreciation that results from things such as (1) changes in zoning laws or other government restrictions, (2) proximity to undesirable influences such as traffic, airport flight patterns, or power lines, and (3) general neighborhood deterioration, as might result from increased crime.

Fair Housing Act — *see*, Civil Rights Act of 1968

false promise — a promise made without any intention of performing it.

Fannie Mae — a U.S. government conservatorship originally created as the Federal National Mortgage Association in 1938 to purchase mortgages from primary lenders.

federally designated targeted area — federally designated locations where homeownership is encouraged and incentivized.

fee simple absolute estate — the greatest estate that the law permits in land. The owner of a fee simple absolute estate owns all present and future interests in the property.

fee simple defeasible estate — a fee estate that is qualified by some condition that, if violated, may "defeat" the estate and lead to its loss and reversion to the grantor.

FHA — the Federal Housing Administration is a federal agency that was created by the National Housing Act of 1934 in order to make housing more affordable by increasing home construction, reducing unemployment, and making home mortgages more available and affordable.

FHFA — the Federal Housing Finance Agency is a U.S. government agency created by the Housing and Economic Recovery Act of 2008 to oversee the activities of Fannie Mae and Freddie Mac in order to strengthen the secondary mortgage market.

FICO score — a credit score created by the Fair Isaac Corporation that ranges from 300 to 850 and is used by lenders to help evaluate the creditworthiness of a potential borrower.

fiduciary relationship — a relationship in which one owes a duty of utmost care, integrity, honesty, and loyalty to another.

final map —a final map that a planning commission must approve after consideration of a tentative map before regulated subdivided property may be sold.

final public report — a report that the Real Estate Commissioner issues after determining that a subdivision offering meets certain consumer protection standards.

finder — a person who merely introduces a buyer to a seller, but does nothing else to facilitate a transaction between the buyer and seller, such as rendering assistance in negotiating terms.

fire stop — a block or board placed horizontally between studs to form a tight closure of a concealed space, thereby decreasing drafts and retarding the spread of fire and smoke.

first mortgage — a security instrument that holds first-priority claim against certain property identified in the instrument.

fixed lease — a gross lease

fixture — an object, originally personal property, that is attached to the land in such a manner as to be considered real property.

flashing — sheet metal or other material used in roof and wall construction to prevent water from entering.

flat fee listing — a listing in which the broker's compensation is a set amount rather than a percentage of the sale price.

floodplain — an area of low, flat, periodically flooded land near streams or rivers.

flue — a channel in a chimney through which flame and smoke passes upward to the outer air.

footing — concrete poured on solid ground that provides support for the foundation, chimney, or support columns. Footing should be placed below the frost line to prevent movement.

forbearance — the act of refraining from taking some action.

foreclosure — a legal process by which a lender, in an attempt to recover the balance of a loan from a borrower who has defaulted on the loan, forces the sale of the collateral that secured the loan.

foreclosure prevention alternative — a first lien loan modification or another available loss mitigation option.

Foreign Investment in Real Property Tax Act (FIRPTA) — a federal act that, with certain exceptions, requires the buyer in a real estate transaction to determine whether the seller is a non-resident alien; and if so, the buyer has the responsibility of withholding 10% of the amount realized from the sale and sending that 10% of the IRS.

Form Report — *see,* Summary Report.

four unities — refers to the common law rule that a joint tenancy requires unity of possession, time, interest, and title.

Freddie Mac — a U.S. government conservatorship originally created as the Federal Home Loan Mortgage Corporation in 1968 to purchase mortgages from primary lenders.

freehold estate — an estate in land whereby the holder of the estate owns rights in the property for an indefinite duration.

front-end ratio — the ratio of monthly housing expenses to monthly gross income.

fully amortized loan — a loan whereby the installment payments are sufficient to pay off the entire loan by the end of the loan term.

fully indexed rate — on an adjustable-rate mortgage, the index plus the margin.

functional obsolescence — depreciation that results (1) from deficiencies arising from poor architectural design, out-dated style or equipment, and changes in utility demand, such as for larger houses with more garage space, or (2) from over-improvements, where the cost of the improvements was more than the addition to market value.

gable roof — a roof with two sloping sides but not sloping ends.

gambrel roof — a roof sloped on two sides, each side having a steep lower slope and a flatter upper slope.

Garn-St. Germain Act — a federal law that made enforceability of due-on-sale provisions a federal issue.

general agent — an agent who is authorized by a principal to act for more than a particular act or transaction. General agents are usually an integral part of an ongoing business enterprise.

general lien — a lien that attaches to all of a person's nonexempt property.

general partnership — a partnership in which each partner has the equal right to manage the partnership and has personal liability for all of the partnership debts.

general plan — a comprehensive, long-term plan for the physical development of a city or county that is implemented by zoning, building codes, and other laws or actions of the local governments.

gift deed — a deed used to convey title when no tangible consideration (other than "affection") is given. The gift deed is valid unless it was used to defraud creditors, in which case such creditors may bring an action to void the deed.

Ginnie Mae — the Government National Mortgage Association is a wholly owned U.S. government corporation within HUD to guarantee pools of eligible loans that primary lenders issue as Ginnie Mae mortgage-backed securities.

good-faith improver — a person who, because of a mistake of law or fact, makes an improvement to land in good faith and under erroneous belief that he or she is the owner of the land.

goodwill — an intangible asset derived from the expectation of continued public patronage.

graduated lease — a lease that is similar to a gross lease except that it provides for periodic increases in rent, often based on the Consumer Price Index.

grantee — one who acquires an interest in real property from another.

grantor — one who transfers an interest in real property to another.

gross income — total income from a property before any expenses are deducted.

gross income multiplier (GIM) — a number equal to the estimated value of a property divided by the gross income of the property.

gross lease — a lease under which the tenant pays a fixed rental amount, and the landlord pays all of the operating expenses for the premises.

gross rent multiplier (GRM) — a number equal to the estimated value of a property divided by the gross rental income of the property.

ground lease — a lease under which a tenant leases land and agrees to construct a building or to make other significant improvements on the land.

group action — in antitrust law, two or more persons agreeing to act in a certain way.

group boycott — in antitrust law, the action of two or more brokers agreeing not to deal with another broker or brokers.

heir — a person entitled to obtain property through intestate succession.

hip roof — a sloping roof that rises from all four sides of the house.

holographic will — a will written, dated, and signed by a testator in his or her own handwriting.

home equity line of credit (HELOC) — a revolving line of credit provided by a home equity mortgage.

home equity mortgage — a security instrument used to provide the borrower with a revolving line of credit based on the amount of equity in the borrower's home.

homeowner's exemption — and exemption of $7,000 from the assessed value of a homeowner's residence.

Homeowner's Protection Act (HPA) — a federal law that requires lenders to disclose to borrowers when the borrowers' mortgages no longer require PMI.

homestead declaration —a recorded document that claims a particular dwelling (such as a house, condominium, boat, or mobile home) as the owner's principal place of residence and that provides limited protection for the claimant's equity in the dwelling.

homestead exemption — the amount of a homeowner's equity that may be protected from unsecured creditors.

horizontal property act — a law that provides for the creation of condominiums and establishes regulations regarding the condominiums and the condominium owners.

HUD-1 Uniform Settlement Statement — an escrow settlement form mandated by RESPA for use in all escrows pertaining to the purchase of owner-occupied residences of 1-4 dwelling units that use funds from institutional lenders regulated by the federal government.

implication — the act of creating an agency relationship by an unauthorized agent who acts as if he or she is the agent of a principal, and this principal reasonably believes that the unauthorized agent is acting as his or her actual agent.

implied contract— a contract not expressed in words, but, through action or inaction, understood by the parties.

implied easement — an easement arising by implication, as when a purchaser of mineral rights automatically acquires an implied right to enter the property to extract the minerals.

impound account — *see*, reserve account

inclusionary zoning — a zoning law that requires builders to set aside a specific portion of new construction for people of low to moderate incomes.

income approach — an appraisal approach that estimates the value of an income-producing property as being worth the present value of the future income of the property through a three-step process: (1) determine the net annual income, (2) determine an appropriate capitalization rate, and (3) divide the net income by the capitalization rate to obtain the estimate of value.

incurable depreciation — depreciation that results from (1) physical deterioration or functional obsolescence that cannot be repaired at a cost that is less than or equal to the value added to the property and (2) economic obsolescence (which is beyond the control of the property owner).

independent contractor — a person who performs work for someone, but does so independently in a private trade, business, or profession, with little or no supervision from the person for whom the work is performed.

index — under an adjustable-rate mortgage, the benchmark rate of interest that is adjusted periodically according to the going rate of T-bills, LIBOR, or the like.

innocent landowner defense — a defense to liability for cleanup of toxic waste under CERCLA (the Superfund Law) by one who acquires contaminated property after the contamination occurred and who acquired the property by inheritance or bequest or who, prior to purchasing the property, performed "all appropriate inquiries" to determine that the property had not been contaminated.

installment note — a promissory note in which periodic payments are made, usually consisting of interest due and some repayment of principal.

installment sale — a sale in which the seller receives at least one payment in a later tax period and may report part of the gain from the sale for the year in which a payment is received.

integration — the growth and development stage of property.

intentional misrepresentation — the suggestion, as a fact, to a party that which is not true committed by another party who does not believe it to be true and who makes the suggestion with the intent to deceive the first party, who was deceived to his or her detriment, such as by being induced to enter into a contract.

interest — the compensation fixed by the parties for the use of money.

interest-rate cap —under an adjustable-rate mortgage, the maximum that the interest rate can increase from one adjustment period to the next or over the life of the entire loan.

interpleader — an action that allows for a neutral third party (such as a real estate agent) to avoid liability to two or more claimants (such as a seller and buyer) to the same money or property (such as an earnest money deposit) by forcing the claimants to litigate among themselves, letting the court determine who deserves what while not enmeshing the neutral third party in the litigation.

Interstate Land Sales Full Disclosure Act — a federal consumer protection act that requires that certain land developers register with the Consumer Financial Protection Bureau if they offer across state lines parcels in subdivisions containing 100 or more lots. Subdivisions where each lot in the subdivision contains at least 20 acres are exempt from this registration requirement. A developer must provide each prospective buyer with a Property Report that contains pertinent information about the subdivision and that discloses to the prospective buyer that he or she has a minimum of 7 days in which to rescind the purchase agreement.

intestate — not having made, or not having disposed of by, a will.

intestate succession — transfer of the property of one who dies intestate.

inverse condemnation — a judicial or administrative action brought by a landowner to force the condemnation of the landowner's land where nearby condemned land or land used for public purposes (such as for noisy airports) severely reduces the value of the landowner's land.

involuntary lien — a lien created by operation of law, not by the voluntary acts of the debtor.

jamb — the vertical sides of a door or window that contact the door or sash.

joint ownership — ownership of property by two or more persons.

joint tenancy —a form of joint ownership which has unity of possession, time, interest, and title.

joist — one of a series of parallel heavy horizontal timbers used to support floor or ceiling loads.

Jones v. Mayer — a landmark 1968 United States Supreme Court case that held that the Civil Rights Act of 1866 was constitutional and that the Act prohibited all racial discrimination, whether private or public, in the sale or rental of property.

judicial foreclosure — a foreclosure carried out not by way of a power-of-sale clause in a security instrument, but under the supervision of a court.

judgment — a court's final determination of the rights and duties of the parties in an action before it.

jumbo loan — a mortgage loan the amount of which exceeds conforming loan limits set by the FHFA on an annual basis.

junior mortgage — a mortgage that, relative to another mortgage, has a lower lien-priority position.

land contract — a real property sales contract.

land installment contract — a real property sales contract.

lateral support — the support that soil receives from the land adjacent to it.

lease extension — a continuation of tenancy under the original lease.

lease-option — a lease (also referred to as a lease with an option to purchase) that provides the tenant with the right, but not the obligation, to purchase the leased property at a specified price within a specified period of time.

lease-purchase — an agreement (also referred to as a lease with an obligation to purchase) that provides for the purchase of property preceded by a lease under which a portion of each lease payment is applied to the purchase price.

lease renewal — a continuation of tenancy under a new lease.

leasehold estate — a less-than-freehold estate.

legatee — one who acquires personal property under a will.

lessee — a person (the tenant) who leases property from another.

lessor — a person (the landlord) who leases property to another.

less-than-freehold estate — an estate in which the holder has the exclusive right to possession of land for a length of time. The holder of a less-than-freehold estate is usually referred to as a lessee or tenant.

level payment note — a promissory note under which all periodic installment payments are equal.

leverage — a method of multiplying gains (or losses) on investments by using borrowed money to acquire the investments.

license to use —a personal right to use property on a nonexclusive basis. A license to use is not considered an estate.

lien —an encumbrance against real property that is used to secure a debt and that can, in most cases, be foreclosed.

lien priority — the order in which lien holders are paid if property is sold to satisfy a debt.

lien stripping — a method sometimes used in Chapter 13 bankruptcies to eliminate junior liens on the debtor's home.

lien theory — a legal theory of mortgage, holding that the mortgagor retains both legal and equitable title of the property, including exclusive possession and use of the property. The mortgagee simply possesses a lien against the property (usually a lien of higher priority than certain other liens, such as judgment liens). Upon default, the mortgagee must go through a formal (judicial) foreclosure proceeding to obtain legal title and possession.

life estate — a freehold estate the duration of which is measured by the life of a natural person — either by the life of the person holding the estate, or by the life or lives of one or more other persons.

limited liability partnership — a partnership in which there is at least one general partner and one or more limited partners. The limited partners have no liability beyond their investment in and pledges to the partnership.

lintel — a horizontal support made of wood, stone, concrete, or steal that lies across the top of a window or door and supports the load above.

liquidated damages — a sum of money that the parties agree, usually at the formation of a contract, will serve as the exact amount of damages that will be paid upon a breach of the contract.

lis pendens — (Latin for "action pending") a notice of pendency of action.

listing agreement — a written contract between a real estate broker and a property owner (the principal) stipulating that in exchange for the real estate broker's procuring a buyer for the principal's property, the principal will compensate the broker, usually with a percentage of the selling price.

loan flipping — the practice of frequently refinancing loans that result in little more than the generation of additional loan fees.

loan modification — a restructuring or modification of a mortgage or deed of trust on terms more favorable to the buyer's ability (or desire) to continue making loan payments.

loan servicing — the administration of a loan from the time the loan proceeds are dispersed to the time the loan is paid off in full.

loan-to-value ratio (LTV) — the amount of a first mortgage divided by the lesser of (1) the appraised value of the property or (2) the purchase price of the property.

long-term capital gain — the capital gain on the sale of a capital asset that was held for a relatively long period of time, usually more than one year.

lot, block, and tract land system — (see " recorded map or plat system ")

maker — the person who makes a promissory note.

margin — a number of percentage points, usually fixed over the life of the loan, that is added to the index of an adjustable-rate mortgage to arrive at the fully indexed rate.

market allocation — in antitrust law, the process of competitors agreeing to divide up geographic areas or types of products or services they offer to customers.

market price — the price actually paid for a particular property.

market value — as defined for appraisal purposes by HUD/FHA is: "The most probable price which a property should bring in a competitive and open market under all conditions requisite to a fair sale, the buyer and seller, each acting prudently, knowledgeably and assuming the price is not affected by undue stimulus."

material fact — a fact that is likely to affect the decision of a party as to whether to enter into a transaction on the specified terms.

mechanics lien — a specific lien claimed by someone who furnished labor or materials for a work of improvement on real property and who has not been fully paid.

median price per square foot — the median price per square foot of a set of properties is the price per square foot of the property whose price per square foot is such that half of the properties in the set have an equal or lower price per square foot and half have an equal or higher price per square foot.

Megan's Law — an informal name for various federal and state laws that provide for the registration of sex offenders and for the making available to the public information regarding the location of these offenders.

menace — a threat to commit duress or to commit injury to person or property.

meridians — (see and compare "base lines")

metes and bounds land description — a method of describing a parcel of land that uses physical features of the locale, along with directions and distances, to define the boundaries of the parcel.

moldings — patterned strips, usually of wood, used to provide ornamental finish to cornices, bases, windows, and door jambs.

mortgage banker — a primary lender that uses its own money in creating a mortgage loan.

mortgage broker — an individual or company that finds borrowers and matches them with lenders for a fee.

mortgagee — a lender or creditor to whom a mortgagor gives a mortgage to secure a loan or performance of an obligation.

mortgage loan originator (MLO) — a person who takes, or offers to take, a residential mortgage loan application or offers or negotiates terms of a residential mortgage application for compensation or gain or in expectation of compensation or gain.

mortgagor — the borrower who gives a mortgage on his or her property to secure a loan or performance of an obligation.

mudsill — for houses built on a concrete slab, the wood sills that are bolted to all sides of the slab, providing a means of attaching portions of the framing for the house to the foundation.

multiple listing service — an organization (MLS) of real estate brokers who share their listings with other members of the organization.

mutual consent — refers to the situation in which all parties to a contract freely agree to the terms of the contract; sometimes referred to as a "meeting of the minds."

National "Do Not Call" Registry — a registry established by the Federal Trade Commission to protect consumers from unwanted commercial telephone solicitations.

National Association of Real Estate Brokers — a real estate trade association whose members are called Realtists®.

National Association of Realtors® — the largest real estate trade association in the United States, founded in 1908, whose members are called Realtors®.

National Environmental Policy Act (NEPA) — a federal law intended to protect, and to promote the enhancement of, the environment.

negative amortization — a loan repayment scheme in which the outstanding principal balance of the loan increases because the installment payments do not cover the full interest due.

negative amortized loan (NegAm loan) — a loan by which the installment payments do not cover all of the interest due — the unpaid part of the interest due being tacked onto the principal, thereby causing the principal to grow as each month goes by.

negative covenant — a contractual promise not to do certain acts, such as build a fence on a property, the remedy for breach thereof being either monetary damages or injunctive relief, not forfeiture.

negative fraud — the act of not disclosing a material fact which induces someone to enter into a contractual relationship and that causes that person damage or loss.

negligent misrepresentation — an assertion not warranted by the information of the party making the assertion that an important fact was true, which was not true, relied on by another party to that party's detriment.

net income — income from a property remaining after expenses are deducted from gross income.

net lease — a lease under which the tenant pays a fixed rental amount plus some of the landlord's operating expenses.

net listing — a listing agreement providing the broker with all proceeds received from the sale over a specified amount. Net listings are not legal in many states.

NMLS — the Nationwide Mortgage Licensing System and Registry is a mortgage licensing system developed and maintained by the Conference of State Bank Supervisors and the American Association of Residential Mortgage Regulators for the state licensing and registration of state-licensed loan originators.

nonconforming loan — a loan not in conformance with FHFA guidelines.

nonconforming use — a zoning exception for areas that are zoned for the first time or that are rezoned and where established property uses that previously were permitted to not conform to the new zoning requirements. As a general rule, such existing properties are "grandfathered in," allowing them to continue the old use but not to extend the old use to additional properties or to continue the old use after rebuilding or abandonment.

non-judicial foreclosure — a foreclosure process culminating in a privately conducted, publicly held trustee's sale. The right to pursue a non-judicial foreclosure is contained in the power-of-sale clause of a mortgage or deed of trust, which, upon borrower default and the beneficiary's request, empowers the trustee to sell the secured property at a public auction.

notice of cessation — a written form that notifies that all work of improvement on a piece of real property has ceased, and that limits the time in which mechanics liens may be filed against the property.

notice of completion — a written form that notifies that a work of improvement on real property has been completed, and that limits the time in which mechanics liens may be filed against the property.

notice of default (NOD) — a document prepared by a trustee at the direction of a lender to begin a non-judicial foreclosure proceeding.

notice of pendency of action — a notice that provides constructive notice to potential purchasers or encumbrancers of a piece of real property of the pendency of a lawsuit in which an interest in that piece of real property is claimed.

notice of sale — a document prepared by a trustee at the direction of a lender that gives notice of the time and place of sale of an identified foreclosed property.

novation — a substitution of a new obligation or contract for an old one, or the substitution of one party to a contract by another, relieving the original party of liability under the contract.

nuisance — anything that is indecent or offensive to the senses, or an obstruction to the free use of property, so as to interfere with the comfortable enjoyment of life or property.

nuncupative will — an oral will.

offer — a proposal by one person (the offeror) to enter into a contract with another (the offeree).

offeree — one to whom an offer to enter into a contract is made.

offeror — one who makes an offer to enter into a contract.

open listing — a listing agreement that gives a broker the nonexclusive right to sell property and receive compensation (usually a commission) if, but only if, the broker is the first to procure a buyer for the property.

opinion of title — a written rendering of an opinion on the condition of ownership of title in a real estate transaction prepared by an attorney after examination of an abstract of title.

option contract — a contract that gives the purchaser of the option the right to buy or lease a certain property at a set price any time during the option term.

ordinary interest — interest calculated by the 30/360 day count convention.

origination fee — the fee a lender charges to cover expenses of processing a loan, such as purchasing credit reports, inspection reports and appraisals, and paying office expenses and salaries of personnel who interview borrowers and analyze the reports and appraisals.

ostensible agency — an agency in which the principal intentionally, or by want of ordinary care, causes a third person to believe another to be his agent who was not actually employed by him.

parol evidence rule — a rule of evidence that prohibits the introduction of extrinsic evidence of preliminary negotiations, oral or written, and of contemporaneous oral evidence, to alter the terms of a written agreement that appears to be whole.

partially amortized loan — an installment loan under which monthly payments pay all of the interest due but not enough of the principal to fully pay off the loan at the end of the loan term. In such a case, a balloon payment would be due at the end of the loan term.

partial release clause — a clause in a blanket mortgage that allows a developer to sell off individual parcels and pay back, according to a release schedule, only a proportionate amount of the blanket loan.

partition — a court-ordered or voluntary division of real property held in joint ownership into parcels owned in severalty.

passive income — in general, income from either rental activity or from a business in which the taxpayer does not materially participate.

passive investor — an investor who does not actively contribute to the management of the business invested in.

patent, land — an instrument used to convey government land.

payee — the person to whom a promissory note is made out.

payment cap —under an adjustable-rate mortgage, the maximum amount that installment payments may increase from one adjustment period to the next or over the life of the loan.

percentage lease — a lease, often used in shopping centers, under which the tenant typically pays a base rent amount plus a percentage of the gross receipts of the tenant's business.

period of redemption — a period of time after a sheriff's sale in a judicial foreclosure proceeding during which the borrower may redeem his or her property by paying off the entire debt plus costs.

periodic tenancy — an estate from period to period.

physical deterioration — depreciation that results from wear and tear of use and from natural causes.

physical life — the period of time that the property lasts with normal maintenance.

pitch — the degree of inclination or slope of a roof.

plaintiff — the one who brings a lawsuit.

plaster — a mixture of lime or gypsum, sand, water, and fiber that is applied to walls and ceilings and that hardens into a smooth coating.

point of beginning — the fixed starting point in the metes and bounds method of land description.

point — in finance, a point is equal to 1% of the loan amount. The term is used by lenders to measure discount charges and other costs such as origination fees and private mortgage insurance premiums.

police power — the power of a government to impose restrictions on private rights, including property rights, for the sake of public welfare, health, order, and security, for which no compensation need be made.

portfolio loans — loans that primary lenders retain in their own investment portfolios rather than sell into the secondary market.

post-dated check — a check dated with a date after the date the check is written and signed.

potentially responsible party — as defined by the EPA, anyone who ever owned or operated a contaminated property, as well as anyone who produced the waste, transported the waste to the property, or disposed of the waste on the property.

power of attorney — a special written instrument that gives authority to an agent to conduct certain business on behalf of the principal. The agent acting under such a grant is sometimes called an attorney in fact.

power-of-sale clause — a clause contained in most trust deeds that permits the trustee to foreclose on, and sell, the secured property without going to court.

preapproval —an evaluation of a potential borrower's ability to qualify for a loan that involves a credit check and verification of income and debt of the potential borrower.

predatory lending — the imposition of unfair, deceptive, abusive, or fraudulent loan terms on borrowers.

prepayment penalty — a fee charged to a borrower for paying off the loan faster than scheduled payments call for.

prequalification — an initial unverified evaluation of a potential borrower's ability to qualify for a mortgage loan.

prescription — a method of acquiring an interest in property by use and enjoyment for five years.

prescriptive easement — an easement acquired by prescription.

price fixing — an agreement between competitors to set prices or price ranges.

price per square foot — the price per square foot of a specific property is determined by dividing the price (either selling or listing) by the property's square footage. Appraisers determine the square footage of a property by using the *outside* measurement of the property.

primary financing — first mortgage property financing.

primary lender — lenders who originate mortgage loans.

primary mortgage market — the market where mortgage loans are originated.

principal — the one whom an agent represents.

principle of anticipation — principle that value is derived from a calculation of anticipated future benefits to be derived from the property, not from past benefits, though past benefits may inform as to what might be expected in the future.

principle of balance — principle that the maximum value of property, its highest and best use, is created and maintained when land use by interacting elements of production are in equilibrium or balance.

principle of change — principle that property values are in a constant state of flux due to economic, environmental, political, social, and physical forces in the area.

principle of competition — principle that increased competition results in increased supply in relation to demand, and thereby to lower profit margins.

principle of conformity — principle that the maximum value of land is achieved when there is a reasonable degree of social, economic, and architectural conformity in the area.

principle of contribution — principle that improvements made to a property will contribute to its value or that, conversely, the lack of a needed improvement will detract from the value of the property.

principle of four-stage life cycle — principle that property goes through a process of growth, stability, decline, and revitalization.

principle of plottage — states that assembling two or more parcels of land into one parcel results in the larger parcel having a greater value than the sum of the values of the smaller parcels.

principle of progression — principle that the value of a residence of less value tends to be enhanced by proximity to residences of higher value.

principle of regression — principle that the value of a residence of higher value tends to be degraded by the proximity to residences of lower value.

principle of substitution — principle that the value of a property will tend toward the cost of an equally desirable substitute property.

principle of supply and demand — principle that the value of property in a competitive market is influenced by the relative levels of supply and demand: the greater level of demand in relation to the level of supply, the greater the value.

principle of the highest and best use — principle that the best use of a property in terms of value is the use most likely to produce the greatest net return (in terms of money or other valued items).

private mortgage insurance (PMI) — mortgage insurance that lenders often require for loans with an LTV more than 80%.

privity of contract — a legal doctrine that states that a legally enforceable relationship exists between the persons who are parties to a contract.

privity of estate — a legal doctrine that states that a legally enforceable relationship exists between the parties who hold interests in the same real property.

probate — a legal procedure whereby a superior court in the county where the real property is located or where the deceased resided oversees the distribution of the decedent's property.

procuring cause — a common law legal concept developed by the courts to determine the proportioning of commissions among agents involved in a real estate transaction In general, an agent who is a procuring cause of a sale originated a chain of events that resulted in the sale and is thereby entitled to at least some part of the total commission generated by the sale.

profit á prendre — the right to enter another's land for such purposes as to drill for oil, mine for coal, or cut and remove timber.

promissory note — a contract whereby one person unconditionally promises to pay another a certain sum of money, either at a fixed or determinable future date or on demand of the payee.

property disclosure statement — a statement filled out by the seller of residential property consisting of 1 to 4 dwelling units, disclosing to potential purchasers defects in the property that are known to the seller, or that should be known to the seller upon reasonable inspection.

proration — an adjustment of expenses that either have been paid or are in arrears in proportion to actual time of ownership as of the closing of escrow or other agreed-upon date.

protected class — a group of people protected from discrimination by federal or state law.

protection clause — *see*, safety clause.

public dedication — a gift of an interest in land to a public body for public use, such as for a street, a park, or an easement to access a beach.

public grant — public land conveyed, usually for a small fee, to individuals or to organizations, such as to railroads or universities.

puffing — the act of expressing a positive opinion about something to induce someone to become a party to a contract.

purchase money loan — a deed of trust or mortgage on a dwelling for not more than four families given to a lender to secure repayment of a loan which was in fact used to pay all or part of the purchase price of that dwelling, occupied entirely or in part by the purchaser.

pyramid roof a hip roof that has no ridge.

quantity survey method — the most detailed method of estimating the replacement or reproduction cost of a structure, in which an estimate is made of the cost of all of the raw materials needed to replace the building. Such material-cost information is available in construction cost handbooks

quiet title action — *see*, suit to quiet title

quitclaim deed — a deed that contains no warranties of any kind, no after-acquired title provisions, and provides the grantee with the least protection of any deed; it merely provides that any interest (if there is any) that the grantor has in the property is transferred to the grantee.

rafter — one of a series of parallel sloping timbers that extend from the ridgeboard to the exterior walls, providing support for the roof.

ratification —the act of creating an agency relationship by a principal who accepts or retains the benefit of an act made by an unauthorized agent.

real estate investment trust (REIT) — a company that invests in and, in most cases operates, income-producing real estate and that meets numerous criteria, such as the necessity of being jointly owned by at least 100 persons.

real estate owned (REO) — property acquired by a lender through a foreclosure sale.

real estate professional — a real estate investor who (1) materially participates for at least 750 hours during the tax year in the real estate business and (2) spends more than 50% of his or her personal services performed in all businesses during the tax year in the real estate business that he or she materially participates in.

Real Estate Settlement Procedures Act (RESPA) — a federal law designed to prevent lenders, real estate agents, developers, title insurance companies, and other agents (such as appraisers and inspectors) who service the real estate settlement process from providing kickbacks or referral fees to each other, and from facilitating bait-and-switch tactics.

real property sales contract — an agreement in which one party agrees to convey title to real property to another party upon the satisfaction of specified conditions set forth in the contract and that does not require conveyance of title within one year from the date of formation of the contract.

Realtist® — a member of the National Association of Real Estate Brokers.

Realtor® — a member of the National Association of Realtors®.

reconciliation — the process of ascertaining value by comparing and evaluating values obtained from comparables or from different valuation approaches; the process of comparing what is in a trust fund account with what should be in the account.

reconveyance deed — a deed executed by the trustee of a deed of trust after the promissory note is paid off in full by the borrower and the lender instructs the trustee to so execute the reconveyance deed, which reconveys legal title to the borrower

recorded map or plat system — a method of land description that states a property's lot, block, and tract number, referring to a map recorded in the county where the property is located.

rectangular survey system — a method of land description based on a grid system of north-south lines ("ranges") and east-west lines ("tier" or "township" lines) that divides the land into townships and sections.

red flag — a condition that should alert a reasonably attentive person of a potential problem that warrants further investigation. Examples include stains on ceilings or walls, the smell of mold, and warped floors or walls.

redlining — the illegal practice of refusing to make loans for real property in particular areas.

Regulation Z — the set of regulations that implement the Truth-in-Lending Act (TILA).

reinforced concrete — concrete poured around steel bars or metal netting to increase its ability to withstand tensile, shear, and compression stresses.

rejection — the act of an offeree that terminates an offer. An offer may be rejected (1) by submitting a new offer, (2) by submitting what purports to be an acceptance but is not because it contains a variance of a material term of the original offer, or (3) by express terms of rejection.

rejuvenation — the phase when a property is rebuilt, remodeled, or otherwise revitalized to a new highest and best use.

reliction — a natural process by which the owner of riparian or littoral property acquires additional land that has been covered by water but has become permanently uncovered by the gradual recession of water.

remainder — the residue of a freehold estate where, at the end of the estate, the future interest arises in a third person.

remainder depreciation — depreciation that will occur after the date of valuation.

remainderman — a person who inherits or is entitled to inherit property held as a life estate when the person whose life determines the duration of the life estate passes away.

replacement cost — the cost of replacing improvements with those having equivalent utility, but constructed with modern materials, designs, and workmanship.

reproduction cost — the cost of replacing improvements with exact replicas at current prices.

request for a reconveyance — an instrument that a lender sends to a trustee requesting that the trustee execute and record a deed of reconveyance that is then sent to the borrower.

rescission — the cancellation of a contract and the restoration of each party to the same position held before the contract was entered into.

reserve account — in reference to loan servicing, the escrow account from which the loan servicer typically pays, on behalf of the borrower, property taxes, hazard insurance, and any other charges (such as mortgage insurance) with respect to the loan.

residual value — an estimate of the reasonable fair market value of a property at the end of its useful life.

respondeat superior — in agency law, the doctrine that a principal is liable for the acts of an agent if those acts were performed within the scope of the agent's authority. (See, vicarious liability.)

retaliatory eviction — an eviction action brought to retaliate against a tenant for making a habitability complaint or for asserting other of the tenant's legal rights.

return on investment (ROI) — an investor's cash flow (net income minus financing charges) divided by the investor's actual cash investment (as distinct from the purchase price).

reverse mortgage — a security instrument for a loan for homeowners over the age of 62 who have a large amount of equity in their homes, usually designed to provide such homeowners with monthly payments, often over the lifetime of the last surviving homeowner who either moves out of the house or dies.

reversion — the residue of a freehold estate where at the end of the estate, the future interest reverts to the grantor.

revocation — the withdrawal of an offer by the person who made the offer.

rezoning amendment — an amendment to a zoning ordinance that property owners may request if they feel that their area has been improperly zoned.

ridgeboard — a horizontal board placed on edge at the apex of a roof to which the upper ends of the rafters are attached.

right of first refusal — the right to be given the first chance to purchase a property at the same price, terms, and conditions as is offered to third parties if and when the property is put up for sale.

right of survivorship — the right to succeed to the interest of a joint tenant or, if community property with right of survivorship, to succeed to the interest of a spouse or registered domestic partner. Right of survivorship is the most important characteristic of joint tenancy.

riparian rights — the rights of a landowner to use water from a stream or lake adjacent to his or her property, provided such use is reasonable and does not injure other riparian owners.

robocall — a pre-recorded, auto-dialed telephone call.

R-value — a measure of the resistance of insulation to heat transfer. The FTC requires sellers of new homes to disclose the R-value of each home's insulation. The higher the R-value, the greater is the effectiveness of the insulation.

SAFE Act — the Safe and Fair Enforcement for Mortgage Licensing Act of 2008 was designed to improve consumer protection and reduce mortgage fraud by setting minimum standards for the licensing and registration of mortgage loan originators.

safety clause — a provision in a listing agreement, providing that the broker will earn the full commission if the property is sold within a specified number of days after the termination of the listing to a buyer with whom the broker has dealt in certain specified ways regarding the property.

sales comparison approach — an appraisal approach that compares recent sales of similar properties in the area to evaluate the market value of the subject property.

salesperson — a natural person who is employed by a licensed real estate broker to perform acts that require having a real estate license.

salvage value — residual value.

sandwich lease — a leasehold interest that lies between a primary lease and a sublease.

sash — frames that contain one or more windowpanes.

scarcity — a lack of abundance.

scrap value — residual value.

second mortgage — a security instrument that holds second-priority claim against certain property identified in the instrument.

secondary financing — second mortgage and junior mortgage property financing

secondary mortgage market — the market where mortgages are sold by primary mortgage lenders to investors.

secret profit — any compensation or beneficial gain realized by an agent not disclosed to the principal. Real estate agents must always disclose any interest that they or their relatives have in a transaction and obtain their principals' consent.

section — one square mile, containing 640 acres.

security instrument — the written instrument by which a debtor pledges property as collateral to secure a loan.

SEER — (see EER)

self-help eviction — a landlord's denial of possession of leased premises to a tenant without complying with the legal process of eviction.

seller carry back loan — a loan or credit given by a seller of real property to the purchaser of that property.

seller's agent — a real estate broker appointed by the seller to represent the seller.

selling agent — the real estate agent who sells or finds and obtains a buyer for the property in a real estate transaction.

senior mortgage — a mortgage that, relative to another mortgage, has a higher lien-priority position.

separate property — property that is owned in severalty by a spouse or registered domestic partner. Separate property includes property acquired before marriage or the registering of domestic partnership, and property acquired as a gift or by inheritance during marriage or registered domestic partnership.

servient tenement — land that is burdened by an easement.

setback — a designation of a governing body as to how far a structure must be situated from something else, such as a curb or a neighboring property.

settlement — *see*, closing

severalty — ownership of property by one person.

severance — the act of detaching an item of real property that changes the item to personal property, such as the cutting down of a natural tree. Also, the act of terminating a relationship, such as the act of partitioning by court order for the transfer of an interest that changes a joint tenancy into a tenancy in common.

severance damages — damages paid to an owner of land partially taken by eminent domain where the value of the remaining portion of the owner's land is severely reduced by the severance of the condemned a portion of owner's land.

sheriff's deed — a deed given at the foreclosure of a property, subsequent to a judgment for foreclosure of a money judgment against the owner or of a mortgage against the property. A sheriff's deed contains no warranties and transfers only the former owner's interest in the property.

sheriff's sale — a sale of property following a judicial foreclosure.

Sherman Act — the federal law passed in 1890 that prohibits agreements, verbal or written, that have the effect of restraining free trade.

short sale — a pre-foreclosure sale made by the borrower (usually with the help of a real estate agent) with lender approval of real estate for less than the balance due on the mortgage loan.

short-term capital gain — the capital gain on the sale of a capital asset that was held for a relatively short period of time, usually one year or less.

sill — the board or metal forming the lower side of the frame for a window or door; the lowest part of the frame of a house, resting on the foundation and providing the base for the studs.

simple interest — the type of interest that is generated only on the principal invested.

single agent — an agent who represents only one party in a given transaction.

single point of contact — an individual or team of personnel employed by a mortgage loan servicer, each of whom has the ability and authority to assist a borrower in assessing whether the borrower may be able to take advantage of a foreclosure prevention alternative offered by, or through, the mortgage servicer.

situs — the legal location of something; also refers to the preference for a particular location to live, work, or invest in

special agent — an agent for a particular act or transaction.

special assessment — a tax levied against properties in a particular area that are benefited by improvements such as for streets, water, and sewers.

specific lien — a lien that attaches only to specific property.

specific performance — a court order that requires a person to perform according to the terms of a contract.

spot zoning —refers to the zoning of isolated properties for use different from the uses specified by existing zoning laws. To spot zone a particular property may, in some cases, be a violation of the requirement that police power apply similarly to all property similarly situated, which in turn arises from the constitutional guarantee of equal protection under the law.

square-foot method — the most widely used method of estimating reproduction or replacement cost of a building, involving the collection cost data on recently constructed similar buildings and dividing the total cost by the square footage to obtain cost per square foot

standard subdivision — is a subdivision with no common areas of ownership or use among the owners of the subdivision parcels.

standby loan commitment — a commitment by a lender to make a take-out loan after construction on a property is completed

statute of frauds — a law that requires certain types of contracts, including most real estate contracts, to be in writing and signed by the party to be bound in order for the contract to be enforceable.

statute of limitations — a law that requires particular types of lawsuits to be brought within a specified time after the occurrence of the event giving rise to the lawsuit.

steering — the illegal practice of directing people of protected classes away from, or toward, housing in particular areas.

stigmatized property — a property having a condition that certain persons may find materially negative in a way that does not relate to the property's actual physical condition.

stock cooperative — a corporation formed or availed of primarily for the purpose of holding title to improved real property either in fee simple or for a term of years.

straight note — a promissory note under which periodic payments consist of interest only.

straight-line depreciation — the expensing of a property by equal amounts over the useful life of the property, determined by subtracting from the cost of the property the estimated residual value of the property and dividing that amount by the useful life of the property measured in years.

straight-line method — a method of calculating annual depreciation of an improvement by dividing the cost of the improvement by the estimated useful life of a typical such improvement.

strict foreclosure — a foreclosure process permitted in a few states, whereby no public sale of the property is made — full title simply passes to the lender.

subagent — an agent of an agent.

subjacent support — the support that soil receives from land beneath it.

subject to — acquiring real property that is burdened by a mortgage without becoming personally liable for the mortgage debt.

subjective value — (also referred to as *value in use*) is value placed on the amenities of a property by a specific person.

sublease — a transfer of a tenant's right to a portion of the leased premises or to the entire premises for less than the entire remaining lease term.

subordination clause — a provision in a mortgage or deed of trust that states that the mortgage or deed of trust will have lower priority than a mortgage or deed of trust recorded later.

subrogation — the substitution of one party for another in regard to pursuing a legal right, interest, or obligation. Subrogation is a legal right used by insurance companies to acquire the right from a policyholder to sue in the place of the policyholder for damages the insurance company paid to the policyholder for some act committed by a third party.

suit to quiet title — a court proceeding intended to establish the true ownership of a property, thereby eliminating any cloud on title.

take-out loan — a loan that provides long-term financing for a property on which a construction loan had been made.

tax assessor — the county or city official who is responsible for appraising property.

tax auditor — the county or city official who maintains the county tax rolls.

tax collector — the county or city official who is responsible for collecting taxes.

tax deed — the deed given to the successful buyer at a tax sale. A tax deed conveys title free and clear from private liens, but not from certain tax liens or special assessment liens, or from easements and recorded restrictions.

tenancy at sufferance — see, estate at sufferance.

tenancy at will — see, estate at will.

tenancy by the entirety — recognized in some states, a special form of joint tenancy between a married couple, in which, as in a joint tenancy, there is the right of survivorship, but in which, unlike in a joint tenancy, neither spouse may convey his or her interest in the property during the lifetime of the other spouse without the consent of the other spouse.

tenancy for years — see, estate for years.

tenancy from period to period — see, estate from period to period.

tenancy in common — a form of joint ownership that is presumed to exist if the persons who own the property are neither married nor registered domestic partners and they own undivided interests in property. Tenants in common may hold unequal interests; however, if the deed does not specify fractional interests among the tenants, the interests will be presumed to be equal.

tenancy in partnership — a form of joint ownership in which the partners combine their assets and efforts in a business venture.

term loan — see, straight loan.

testament — a will.

testator — one who dies leaving a will.

time-share estate — an estate in real property coupled with the right of occupancy for certain periods of time.

time-share use — a right to occupancy during certain periods of time, not coupled to an estate in real property.

title plant — a duplicate of county title records maintained at title insurance companies for use in title searches.

title search — an examination of all relevant public documents to determine whether there exist any potential defects (such as judicial liens, lis pendens, or other encumbrances, including tax liens and special assessments) against the title.

title theory — a legal theory of mortgage, holding that a mortgage transfers legal title to the mortgagee (the lender) while the mortgagor (the borrower) retains equitable title to the property, which permits the mortgagor exclusive possession and use of the property. Upon default, the mortgagee is entitled to immediate possession and use (such as to collect rents) of the property.

townhouse — a form of condominium in which the individual units are connected by a common wall and, in general, (unlike in a high-rise condominium complex) a deed to the land beneath the townhouse is granted to the townhouse owner.

township — six square miles, containing 36 sections.

trade fixtures — objects that a tenant attaches to real property for use in the tenant's trade or business. Trade fixtures differ from other fixtures in that, even though they are attached with some permanence to real property, they may be removed at the end of the tenancy of the business.

transactional broker — a nonagent middleman who brings the parties to a real estate transaction together and lets the parties do all of the negotiating among themselves. States that permit this kind of nonagent-facilitator status impose an obligation on the transactional broker to act fairly, honestly, and competently to find qualified buyers or suitable properties, but the transactional broker does not owe fiduciary legal obligations to any of the parties.

transferability — the ability to transfer some interest in property to another.

triggering term — any of a number of specific finance terms stated in an advertisement for a loan that triggers Regulation Z disclosure requirements in the advertisement.

triple net lease — a lease under which the tenant pays a fixed rent plus the landlord's property taxes, hazard insurance, and all maintenance costs.

trust account — an account set up by a broker at a bank or other recognized depository in the state where the broker is doing business, into which the broker deposits all funds entrusted to the broker by principles or others.

trust deed — a three-party security device, the three parties being the borrower (trustor), the lender (beneficiary), and a third-party (trustee) to whom "bare legal title" is conveyed.

trust fund overage — a situation in which a trust fund account balance is greater than it should be.

trust fund shortage — a situation in which a trust fund account balance is less than it should be.

trustee — a person who holds something of value in trust for the benefit of another; under a deed of trust, a neutral third-party who holds naked legal title for security.

trustor — a borrower who executes a deed of trust.

Truth-in-Lending Act (TILA) — a federal consumer protection law that was enacted in 1968 with the intention of helping borrowers understand the costs of borrowing money by requiring disclosures about loan terms and costs (in particular, the APR) and to standardize the way in which certain costs related to the loan are calculated and disclosed.

tying arrangement — occurs in antitrust law when the seller conditions the sale of one product or service on the purchase of another product or service.

underwriter — one who analyzes the risk of, and recommends whether to approve, a proposed mortgage loan.

undivided interest — an ownership interest in property in which an owner has the right of possession of the entire property and may not exclude the other owners from any portion by claiming that a specific portion of the property is his or hers alone.

undivided interest subdivision — a subdivision in which owners own a partial or fractional interest in an entire parcel of land. The land in an undivided interest subdivision is not divided; its ownership is divided.

unenforceable contract — a contract that a court would not enforce.

Uniform Commercial Code (UCC) — a set of laws that established unified and comprehensive regulations for security transactions of personal property and that superseded existing laws in that field.

unilateral contract — a contract in which one party gives a promise that is to be accepted not by another promise but by performance.

uninformed misrepresentation — *see,* negligent misrepresentation.

unit-in-place method — a method of estimating the replacement or reproduction cost of a structure by calculating the unit cost of components of the structure.

unity of interest — in reference to joint ownership, refers to each of the owners having equal interests in the property.

unity of possession — in reference to joint ownership, refers to each of the owners having an equal, undivided right to possession of the entire property.

unity of time — in reference to joint ownership, refers to each of the owners having acquired his/her interest in the property at the same time.

unity of title — in reference to joint ownership, refers to each of the owners having received ownership in the property from the same deed.

universal agent — an agent given power of attorney to act on behalf of a principal for an unlimited range of legal matters.

unlawful detainer — a legal action to regain possession of real property.

useful life — the estimated period during which a property generates revenue (if the property is an income property) or usefulness (if the property, such as a private residence, has value other than income value).

U.S. government survey system — see rectangular survey system

usury — the charging of interest in excess of that allowed by law.

utility — the usefulness of property; its ability to satisfy a potential buyer's need or desire, such as to provide shelter or income.

VA — the Department of Veterans Affairs is a federal agency designed to benefit veterans and members of their families.

valid contract — a contract that is binding and enforceable in a court of law.

value — the present worth to typical users or investors of all rights to future benefits, arising out of property ownership.

variance — an exception that may be granted in cases where damage to the value of a property from the strict enforcement of zoning ordinances would far outweigh any benefit to be derived from enforcement.

vendee — the purchaser in a real property sales agreement

vendor — the seller in a real property sales agreement.

vicarious liability — liability imposed on a person not because of that person's own acts but because of the acts of another. (See, respondeat superior.)

void contract — a purported contract that has no legal effect.

voidable contract — a contract that, at the request of one party only, may be declared unenforceable, but is valid until it is so declared.

voluntary lien — a lien obtained through the voluntary action of the one against whose property the lien attaches.

warranty deed — a deed in which the grantor warrants that the title being conveyed is good and free from defects or encumbrances, and that the grantor will defend the title against all suits.

warranty of habitability — mandated by both statutes and by common law, an implied warranty in any residential lease that the premises are suitable for human habitation.

wetlands — as defined by the EPA, "areas that are soaked or flooded by surface or groundwater frequently enough or for sufficient duration to support plants, birds, animals, and aquatic life. Wetlands generally include swamps, marshes, bugs, estuaries, and other inland and coastal areas, and are federally protected."

will — a document that stipulates how one's property should be distributed after death; also called a testament.

writ — a court order commanding the person to whom it is directed to perform an act specified therein.

writ of attachment — a writ ordering the seizure of property belonging to a defendant to ensure the availability of the property to satisfy a judgment if the plaintiff wins.

writ of execution — a writ directing a public official (usually the sheriff) to seize and sell property of a debtor to satisfy a debt.

writ of possession — a court order that authorizes the sheriff or other eviction authority to remove a tenant and the tenant's possessions from leased premises.

zoning — laws of a city or county that specify the type of land-use that is acceptable in certain areas.

REAL ESTATE MATH

Section 1: Basic Math Concepts

The only math you are expected to know for the real estate exam is the basic math that will help you solve practical, everyday real estate problems. Memorize a few measurement correspondences, become familiar with a few simple equations and how they apply to practical real estate problems, and you will do just fine.

Here are the measurement correspondences that you should memorize:

- 1 mile = 5,280 feet or 320 rods
- 1 rod = 16½ ft.
- 1 township = 6 mi.× 6 mi. = 36 sections
- 1 section = 1 mi. × 1 mi. = 640 acres
- 1 acre = 43,560 square feet

Converting Decimals, Percentages, and Fractions. Being able to calculate percentages and fractions is of vital importance to real estate agents because commissions, property taxes, interest rates, buyer qualification ratios, loan-to-value ratios, capitalization rates, and gross rent and gross income multipliers all involve working with percentages and fractions.

To convert a percentage to a decimal, simply remove the % sign and move the decimal point two places to the left:

15% → .15

74.6% → .746

To convert a decimal to a percent, move the decimal point two places to the right and add the % sign:

.75 → 75%

1.12 → 112%

To convert a fraction to a decimal, divide the numerator (the number on top) by the denominator (the number on the bottom):

1/5→ 1÷ 5 → .20

3/4→ 3 ÷ 4→ .75

A. Area:

When calculating the area of something (usually expressed in square feet), remember that the area of a rectangle is base × height and the area of a triangle is ½ × base × height.

Example: *Kevin is going to purchase the lot shown in Figure 10 below and build on it a house and garage, also shown in Figure 10. He has been quoted the following: $150 per square foot for the house; $40 per square foot for the garage; $10 per square foot for the land. What is the total amount that Kevin will pay for this lot, house, and garage?*

Answer: First we calculate the square footage of each item:

house area = 60' × 30' = 1,800 ft.²

garage area = 25' × 18' = 450 ft.²

lot area = ½ × 100' × 150' = 7,500 ft.²

cost of house = 1800 ft.² × $150 per ft.² = $270,000

cost of garage = 450 ft.² × $40 per ft.² = $18,000

cost of the lot = 7500 ft.² × $10 per ft.² = $75,000

Total = $363,000

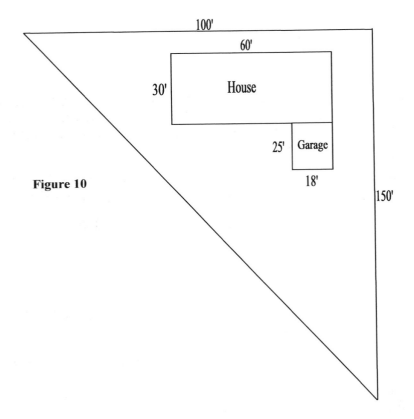

Figure 10

Example: The SW¼ of the SW¼ of the NW¼ of section 10 of Baker Township contains how many square feet?

Answer: A section of a township contains 640 acres. Therefore, ¼ × ¼ × ¼ × 640 acres = 10 acres. Because there are 43,560 square feet per acre, we get 435,600 square feet.

B. Loan-to-Value Ratios:

The **loan-to-value ratio (LTV)** is an important risk factor lenders use to assess the viability of a proposed loan. LTV is defined as the amount of a first mortgage divided by the *lesser* of (1) the appraised value of the property or (2) the purchase price of the property. As a general rule, a high LTV (usually seen as over 80%) will either cause:

- the loan to be denied;
- the lender to increase the cost of the loan to the borrower; or
- the lender to require that the borrower pay for private mortgage insurance.

Example: For a property with an appraised value of $100,000, a sales price of $110,000, and a loan of $90,000, the LTV would be $90,000/$100,000 = 90%.

Example: *If a loan has an LTV of 80%, an appraised value of $120,000, and the sales price of $110,000, what is the amount of the loan?*

Answer: LTV = .8 = loan amount/$110,000.

Therefore, loan amount equals $110,000 × .8 = $88,000.

C. Discount Points:

In finance, a point is equal to 1% of the loan amount. The term is used by lenders to measure charges and other costs such as origination fees and private mortgage insurance premiums. If 1.25 points are charged on a $150,000 loan, the lender would collect 1.25% of $150,000, or $1,875.

Example: *Suppose that Sally is purchasing a house for $250,000 with 20% down. The lender requires 2.5 discount points. How much will Sally pay the lender for the discount points?*

Answer: The loan amount is $250,000 - $50,000 (the down payment) = $200,000.

$200,000 × .025 = $5,000

D. Equity:

Equity is the difference between the current market value of a property and the total indebtedness against the property. If each mortgage payment pays all of the current interest plus some part of the outstanding principal, then the equity increases with each mortgage payment in the amount of the outstanding principal reduction due to the mortgage payment.

Example: Suppose that you have a home with a fair market value $300,000, a first mortgage with outstanding principal of $200,000, and a home equity loan with outstanding principal of $27,000. The equity in your home would be ($300,000 - $200,000) - $27,000 = $73,000.

Home equity loans and home equity lines of credit (HELOC) are loans and lines of credit based on the equity of your home. Typically, these kinds of loans give a loan (or credit line) up to 80% of the appraised value of your home, minus total outstanding indebtedness against the home.

Example: *Joe's home is appraised that $200,000. The first mortgage against his home has an outstanding balance of $100,000. Joe has just arranged to obtain an 80% home equity line of credit of the type described above. What is the amount of his line of credit?*

Answer: ($200,000 × .8) - $100,000 = $60,000.

Note that the answer is NOT ($200,000 - $100,000) × .8 = $80,000.

E. Down Payment/Amount to Be Financed:

A down payment is the amount of money that a lender requires a purchaser to pay toward the purchase price. Note that a down payment is what a lender requires; an earnest money deposit is what a seller requires. The two are different, though an earnest money deposit is often applied toward the down payment.

Example: Andrew is purchasing a home with a purchase price of $300,000 and an appraised value of $290,000. If the lender is willing to loan 80% of the lesser of the purchase price and the appraised value, how much will be Andrew's down payment?

Answer: Loan amount = $290,000 × .8 = $232,000.

Down payment = purchase price - loan amount = $300,000 - $232,000 = $68,000.

Section 2: Calculations for Transactions, Including Mortgage Calculations

Installment loans require periodic payments that include some repayment of principal as well as interest. Installment loans are the most common type of loan used to finance real estate, and the most frequently used installment loan is the *level payment loan* — a loan under which all periodic installment payments are equal, though the amount allocated to principal and interest may vary over the term of the loan. A loan wherein the payments are sufficient to pay off the entire loan by the end of the loan term is referred to as a *fully amortized loan*.

Example: *José purchased a home for $195,130 with a 6% fixed-rate, fully amortized 30-year loan in the principal amount of $156,104. He makes payments of $936 per month. What is the amount of unpaid principal on this loan after the first month's payment?*

Answer: $156,104 × .06 ÷ 12 = $780.52 (first month's interest)

$936 - $780.52 = $155.48 (first month's principal payment)

$156,104 - $155.48 = $155,948.52 (principal balance after first month's payment).

Section 3: Property Tax Calculations

Property taxes are assessed on an *ad valorem* (according to value) basis. The value used is not necessarily the fair market value; rather, it is the assessed value. To find the annual property tax, take the assessed value, subtract any applicable exemption (such as a homestead exemption), and multiply by the annual tax rate.

Example: *A home has a fair market value of $450,000, a homestead exemption of $75,000, an assessed value of $368,000, and a county property tax of 1.2%. What is the annual county property tax on this home?*

Answer: ($368,000 - $75,000) × .012 = $3,516.

Example: *In the above example, what is the amount of tax savings due to the homestead exemption?*

Answer: $75,000 × .012 = $900.

Section 4: Prorations (utilities, rent, property taxes, insurance, etc.)

When calculating proration problems, it is important to know what *day count convention* to use. An exact calculation would take into account the precise number of days: 30 days for some months, 31 or 28 or 29 for other months; 365 days for some years, 366 for leap years. In the days before computers, such calculations would have been quite burdensome, so the *30/360 day count convention* was adopted to simplify certain calculations. When using the 30/360 day count convention, each month is considered to have 30 days, and each year is considered to have 360 days. A year consisting of 360 days with 12 months of 30 days each is often referred to as a *statutory year*, or a *banker's year*. The 30/360 day count convention for calculating *proration, interest, insurance premiums*, and similar expenses is standard in the real estate market. However, in some areas, rules for calculating proration, interest, etc., are based on the actual number of days in a month or year.

Proration questions that appear on your real estate exam will state whether calculations should be based on 360 or 365 days a year, and whether the day of closing belongs to the seller or to the buyer.

A. Commission and Commission Splits:

Because nearly every real estate agent expects to receive commissions (many, hopefully!), it is not unlikely that a question or two relating to commissions might appear on an exam.

Example: *Jessica is a real estate salesperson who found a buyer for a home that sold for $800,000. Jessica's employing broker received a 5% commission for the sale. The agreement between the broker and Jessica provides that she receive 40% of the broker's commission on every sale she procures. What is Jessica's commission on this transaction?*

Answer: Here the solution is to first find the broker's commission:

5% of $800,000 = .05 × $800,000 = $40,000. Jessica is to receive 40% of $40,000 = .40 × $40,000 = $16,000.

Another way to think about such a problem is to note that Jessica receives 40% of 5% = .40 × .05 = .02 = 2% of the sales price. Using this 2% figure, we find that 2% of $800,000 = .02 × $800,000 = $16,000.

Example: *Bob is a salesperson who works for broker Janet. Bob's agreement with Janet is that he gets a commission of 40% of whatever commission Janet receives on sales made by Bob. Bob procures a sale of a house that was listed by broker Susan, who had a cooperating agent agreement with Janet to split the commission on the sale 50-50. Susan's listing agreement with the owner called for a 6% commission. Bob's commission on the sale was $6,000. How much did the house sell for?*

Answer: Because they tend to be long-winded, these types of problems *appear* to involve much more thought than they actually do — they simply need to be approached methodically, step-by-simple-step, until the answer falls out:

The problem tells us that:

$6,000 = 40\%$ of 50% of 6% of Sales Price

$\qquad = (.4 \times .5 \times .06) \times$ Sales Price

$\qquad = .012 \times$ Sales Price (i.e., 1.2% of Sales Price)

Therefore, dividing each side of the equation by .012, we get

$500,000 =$ Sales Price.

B. Seller's Proceeds of Sale:

As a general rule, at the close of escrow in a real estate transaction certain allocations of expenses incurred in the ordinary course of property ownership must be made. For example, if the escrow closes midyear or midmonth, the seller may have prepaid taxes, insurance, or association dues, in which case credit to the seller's account should be made. Conversely, if the seller is behind on paying taxes or insurance, etc., the seller's account should be debited. Such an adjustment of expenses that either have been paid or are in arrears in proportion to actual time of ownership as of the closing or other agreed-upon date is called *proration*. Proration, like ordinary interest, is generally calculated according to the 30/360 day count convention (statutory year).

To compute proration, follow these steps:

1. determine which, if any, expenses are to be prorated;
2. determine to whom the expenses should be credited or debited;
3. determine how many days the expenses are to be prorated;
4. calculate the per day proration amount; and
5. multiply the number of days by the per day proration amount.

Example 12: *Susan purchased a condo for $200,000 that had been rented from Bob at $1,500 a month. Escrow closed on September 16. How should the $200,000 selling price be adjusted at close of escrow if the day of closing belongs to the buyer?*

Answer: Rent is normally collected *in advance* on the first day of the month, so unless stated otherwise one should make this assumption in proration of rent problems. Under this assumption, Bob received $1,500 on or about September 1, but only deserved to keep half of the month's rent because Susan acquired ownership of the condo on September 16. Therefore, Susan should be credited $750 at the close of escrow.

C. Transfer Tax/Conveyance Tax/Revenue Stamps:

Many states tax the transfer of real estate. These taxes are variously referred to as transfer taxes, conveyance taxes, or stamp taxes and are usually imposed either (1) on the total amount of the transfer price (usually less the amount of a loan or other liens the seller had on the property that the buyer assumes responsibility for paying), or (2) imposed on the amount of either assumed mortgages or newly created mortgages.

Example: *A residential property was purchased for $450,000. The state documentary transfer fee is $.55 for each $500 or fraction thereof. The property was purchased with $400,000 cash and an assumption of the $50,000 seller's mortgage. Assumed mortgages are exempt from the transfer fee in this state. What is the documentary transfer fee?*

Answer: $400,000 = 500×800.

$800 \times \$0.55 = \$440$.

D. Amortization Tables:

Although interest and principal payments for loans are now calculated on financial calculators or on calculation software freely available on the Internet, we will look briefly at a simplified amortization table to get a feel for how such a chart was used (in the old days) to calculate the monthly payments for fixed-rate loans at various interest rates. (See Figure 11).

The table displays in the left column the interest rate, and in columns to the right, the term in years of a fixed-rate, fully amortized loan. To find the monthly payment *per $1,000* principal borrowed, simply find the intersection of the rate and term of the loan.

Fig. 11

Monthly Payment Per $1,000 on Fixed-Rate, Fully Amortized Loans				
Rate	10-year term	15-year term	30-year term	40-year term
4%	10.125	7.397	4.775	4.180
5%	10.607	7.908	5.369	4.822
6%	11.102	8.439	5.996	5.503
7%	11.611	8.989	6.653	6.215
8%	12.133	9.557	7.338	6.954

Example: *Susan makes payments of $936 per month, including 6% interest on a fixed-rate, fully amortized 30-year loan. What was the initial amount of her loan?*

Answer: Finding where 6% and a 30-year term intersect in the table, we obtain the number 5.996 which is the dollar amount per month per $1,000 of the initial loan.

$5.996/\$1,000 = \$936/$loan amount. Therefore,

loan amount $= (\$936 \div \$5.996) \times \$1,000 = \$156,104$.

E. Interest Rates:

Interest is the "rent" we pay to possess, use, and enjoy someone else's money. The yearly rent for each dollar we use (borrow) is called the interest rate — if we pay 8¢ each year for each dollar, the interest rate is 8% per year.

Interest problems generally involve four simple concepts:

1. *Interest Rate* (which, to avoid wordiness, we will call Rate);
2. *Principal* (the amount of money borrowed);
3. *Time* (the number of years or fraction of years the principal is borrowed);
4. *Interest Due and Owing* (which we will call Interest).

49

Because the interest due and owing (Interest) is equal to the interest rate (Rate) times the amount of money borrowed (Principal) times the amount of time the money is borrowed (Time),

Interest = Rate × Principal × Time

The above formula is known as *simple interest*, which considers interest to be generated only on the principal invested. A more rapid method of generating interest earnings is referred to as compounding. *Compound interest* is generated when accumulated interest is reinvested to generate interest earnings from previous interest earnings. Though the amount of interest generated can be revved up by compounding yearly, semiannually, quarterly, daily, or even continuously, real estate exams stick with simple interest, as do most real estate loans on which interest is paid monthly. Interest calculated by the 30/360 day count convention is referred to as *ordinary interest*.

Example: *If $6,000 is loaned for one 30-day month on the basis of simple interest, and the total amount of principal and interest due at the end of that month is $6,017.5, what annual rate of interest was charged?*

Answer: $17.50 (interest) = $6,000 (principal) × (annual interest rate/12).
Therefore, annual interest rate = ($17.50 ÷ $6,000) × 12 = 3.5%

F. Interest Amounts:

Example: *What is the interest on a $400,000 loan for 1 year, 2 months, and 10 days at 6% interest (using a statutory year)?*

Answer: The time elapsed is 360 days + 60 days +10 days = 430 days.
430 ÷ 360 = 1.19444 years. Therefore, applying our formula
Interest = Rate × Principal × Time, we get
Interest = .06 × $400,000 × 1.19444 = $28,666.56.

Example: *Jessica borrows $12,000 from her friend Susan. The terms of the loan are that principal will be paid back in equal monthly installments over a five-year period along with the interest that was generated at the annual rate of 6% during the month on the outstanding balance of principal owing. What is Jessica's payment to Susan at the end of the second month?*

Answer: To answer this question, we first have to answer another question; namely, how much principal does Jessica pay Susan at the end of the first month? This is due to the fact that Susan's first month payment will reduce the principal amount on which the second month payment must be calculated.

Because there are 60 months in 5 years, the amount of Susan's monthly payment attributable to principal is $12,000 ÷ 60 = $200. Therefore, the amount of principal owed after the first-month payment is made is $12,000 - $200 = $11,800. Consequently, the second month payment will be $200 + the interest due on $11,800 *for one month*. Because the interest rate is 6% annually, the monthly rate is 1/2%. Thus, the second-month payment is $200 + 1/2% of $11,800 = $259.

G. Monthly Installment Payments:

To obtain the monthly mortgage payment on a level payment loan, the amount of principal and interest is obtained from a loan table (or from a financial calculator) and to this is added 1/12 of the annual property taxes and 1/12 of the home insurance to obtain the PITI (principal, interest, tax, and insurance) payment.

Example: *John and Sandra make monthly mortgage payments of $725.68 for principal and interest. Their annual property taxes are $1,245.30 and their homeowner's insurance is $217 per year. What is their monthly PITI payment?*

Answer: $1,245.30 ÷ 12 = $103.78 tax per month

$217 ÷ 12 = $18.08 insurance per month

Total PITI payment per month = $725.68 + $103.78 + $18.08 = $847.54.

H. Buyer Qualification Ratios:

Prior to approving a loan, a loan processor must obtain information on monthly housing expenses, which the underwriter will use to establish a ratio of monthly housing expenses to monthly gross income, and information on total monthly recurring debt obligations, which the underwriter will use to establish a ratio of total monthly expenses to monthly gross income. Monthly housing expenses include principal, interest, taxes, and insurance (referred to as *PITI*). Total monthly expenses include housing expenses plus additional long-term monthly debt service, such as for car payments, credit card payments, child support, and alimony. In this context, "long-term debt" typically refers to debt that is not scheduled to be retired within 9 months. Monthly housing expenses divided by the monthly gross income is referred to as the *PITI* or *front-end ratio*. Total monthly expenses divided by monthly gross income is referred to as the *LTD* or *back-end ratio*.

For example, suppose that

- monthly gross income = $4,000;
- PITI = $1,000; and
- additional long-term monthly debt expenses = $400.

In this case,

- PITI ratio = $1,000 ÷ $4,000 = 25%
- LTD ratio = $1,400 ÷ $4,000 = 35%

Example: *Sam and Susan's combined monthly gross income is $6,000. What is the maximum PITI they can have to qualify if the lender demands no greater than a 32% PITI ratio?*

Answer: $6,000 × .32 = $1,920.

I. Prepayment Penalties:

A prepayment penalty is a fee charged to a borrower for paying off a loan faster than scheduled payments call for. The penalty is usually calculated as a percentage of a certain number of months of interest on the loan. Therefore, if the borrower has a $200,000 loan with interest at the rate of 4%, and the prepayment penalty is 80% of six months interest, the prepayment payment would be 80% × 4%/year × ½ year × $200,000 = $3,200.

Section 5: Calculations for Valuation

A. Competitive/Comparative Market Analyses (CMA):

We discussed in Chapter 3, Section 3, some of the differences between a comparative market analysis (also referred to as a competitive market analysis) (CMA) and the sales comparison approach to appraisal. However, both the sales comparison approach and a CMA compare in the same manner recent sales of similar local properties to arrive at an estimated market value of a subject property. A detailed example of the sales comparison approach can be found in Chapter 3, Section 2, Figure 5.

The most important thing to keep in mind in a sales comparison appraisal or in a CMA problem is that it is *the values of items of the comparable properties, not the value of items of the subject property, that are adjusted* for differences between the comparables and the subject property. The second most important thing to keep in mind is that if a comparable property has a *superior* feature (such as a better pool) the value of the comparable is adjusted *down* in the amount of the difference between the value of the comparable pool and the value of the subject property pool. On the other hand, had the value of the comparable pool been *less* than the value of the subject pool, the value of the comparable property would have been adjusted *up* accordingly.

Example: *The subject property and a comparable are tract homes that share a common wall. The two houses appear almost exactly the same except that the comparable has an inferior view estimated to be worth $3,000 less than the subject view, and the comparable has superior landscaping estimated to be worth $4,500 more than the subject landscaping. What adjustments should be made?*

Answer: The comparable has a view and landscaping combined value of $1,500 more than the subject view and landscaping value. Therefore, the comparable value should be adjusted down by $1,500.

B. Net Operating Income:

Net operating income (NOI) is determined as follows:

a) estimate the potential annual gross income the property;

b) deduct from the gross income an annual allowance for vacancies and uncollectible rents to arrive at the **effective gross income**; and

c) deduct from the effective gross income the estimate of annual operating expenses, including fixed expenses (such as hazard insurance and real estate taxes), maintenance, and reserves for replacements of building components.

Not all expenses are deducted from effective gross income to obtain net operating income. Examples of such expenses include mortgage payments and taxes on income.

Example: *What is the value of a property based on the following information?*

Estimated potential annual gross income: $95,000

Vacancies and uncollectible rents: 7%

Annual maintenance expenses and utilities: $10,000

Annual property taxes: $9,500

Annual insurances: $1,500

Capitalization rate: 9.5%

Answer: $95,000 × .07 = $6,650 (vacancy and uncollectible rents losses)

$95,000 - $6,650 = $88,350 (effective gross income)

$88,350 - $21,000 (operating expenses) = $67,350 (NOI)

$67,350 ÷ .095 = $708,947 (rounded).

C. Depreciation:

Although many different ways to calculate depreciation are allowed by law (depending on what law one has to satisfy), the only method of depreciation that appears to be tested on real estate license exams is **straight-line depreciation**, which assumes that the property depreciates by an *equal amount* each year.

Depreciation is based on what is considered the **useful life** (also referred to as the **economic life**) of the property and on the estimated **residual value** (also referred to as **salvage value** or **scrap value**) of the property at the end of the property's useful life. Some property, such as computers, have a much shorter useful life than do buildings, so it is always important when considering depreciation to know what the useful life of the item being depreciated is. Straight-line depreciation is defined as:

Annual Depreciation = (Cost of Property - Residual Value) ÷ (useful life in years).

Thus, if the property has a 5-year useful life and no residual value, the rate of (straight-line) depreciation is 100% ÷ 5 years = 20% per year.

Example: *Evan purchases a building for $3,000,000 that has a useful life of 30 years and salvage value of $0. After 10 years, what is the value of the building, if by "value" we mean the original cost less accumulated straight-line depreciation?*

Answer: Here the depreciation rate is: 100% ÷ 30 years = 3⅓ % per year.

3⅓ % per year × 10 years = 33⅓ % depreciation.

33⅓ % of the initial value = 33⅓ % × $3 million = $1 million.

Therefore, value = cost - depreciation = $2,000,000.

Example: If in the above example the land the building was on was worth $750,000, and the question asked for the value of the property after 10 years, the answer would be $2,750,000.

D. Capitalization Rate:

The **capitalization rate** (also referred to as the **cap rate**) is the rate that an appraiser estimates is the yield rate expected by investors from comparable properties in current market conditions. To estimate the capitalization rate of a certain property, an appraiser will collect data on the market value of comparable properties, on the vacancies and uncollectible rents of these comparable properties, and on the operating expenses of these comparable properties. Then, because value = net operating income ÷ capitalization rate, the capitalization rate can be calculated for these comparable properties as net operating income ÷ market value.

Example: *If the annual net operating income of a property is $20,000 and the capitalization rate is 8.5% per year, what would be the value of the property based on an income valuation of the property?*

Answer: $20,000 ÷ 8.5% = $235,294 (rounded).

E. Gross Rent and Gross Income Multipliers (GRM, GIM):

As we have seen, the income approach uses capitalization of *net* operating income to arrive at the valuation of a property. However, some investors, especially of single-family homes, use a simpler method of determining value: capitalization of *gross* income. If only gross rents are capitalized, this approach to value is called the **gross rent multiplier (GRM)** approach; if additional income is involved (such as from parking fees), the method is called the **gross income multiplier (GIM)** approach.

Example: *Using the gross rent multiplier approach, suppose the sales price of a condo is $1,400,000 and the monthly rent is $5,000. What is the monthly gross rent multiplier of this condo?*

Answer: In this case the sales price is $1,400,000 ÷ $5,000 = 280 times the monthly rental; i.e., the monthly gross rent multiplier is 280.

Example: Suppose now that other comparable homes in the area have a monthly gross rent multiplier similar to the home in the prior example. Further, suppose that a comparable home in the area with a fair market value of $900,000 is to be rented. Using the gross rent multiplier approach, what would be the monthly rent for this subject property.

Answer: By dividing the value ($900,000) by the monthly gross rent multiplier (280), we calculate a rent of $3,214 per month.

PRACTICE EXAM #1:

Note: Questions 1-30 of this exam consist of *state-portion* questions of the Pennsylvania real estate exam. Questions 31-110 of this exam consist of *national-portion* questions of the Pennsylvania relics eight exam.

1. The Pennsylvania Seller Property Disclosure Statement requires disclosure of
   a. the primary reason(s) that the seller wishes to sell
   b. the price of comparable homes
   c. all appraisals of the property obtained by the seller in the past 5 years
   (d) the source of drinking water

2. Pennsylvania uses which of the following methods of legal land description?
   a. metes and bounds
   b. lot and block
   (c) both a and b
   d. neither a nor b

3. Joyce conveys her property to her brother John "while" she remains married to Bob. John receives a
   a. fee simple absolute
   (b.) fee simple determinable → no need for court when Joyce passes John will get say w/ her property
   c. fee simple subject to a condition subsequent
   d. life estate

4. Pennsylvania law creates two main categories of life estates. They are
   a. legal life estate and pur autre vie
   b. conventional life estate and pur autre vie
   (c) legal life estate and conventional life estate
   d. dower and curtesy

5. Martha, who lives in Pennsylvania, has for the past 22 years and without Emily's approval tossed her used Christmas tree over their party wall onto Emily's backyard.
   a. Martha has a prescriptive easement
   (b) Martha does not have a prescriptive easement. —Because Emily had no idea
   c. Martha has a license to use.
   d. Martha has acquired an attachment.

55

6. Ruth has a one-year lease for Bob's condo. Ruth is not delinquent on rent payments, but Bob wants his nephew to move into the condo. Under Pennsylvania law, Bob should give Ruth notice to quit at least how many days before the end of the lease term?

   a. 10

   b. 15

   c. 30

   d. 60

7. Unless another form of co-ownership is specified, when a husband and wife take title to Pennsylvania real estate, they take the property as

   a. separate property

   b. community property

   c. tenants-in-common

   d. tenants by the entireties

8. Under the Pennsylvania Mechanics' Lien Law, a contractor or subcontractor must file a claim for a mechanic's lien within how many months of completion of his work?

   a. Six months

   b. Four months

   c. Two months

   d. One year

9. A Pennsylvania commercial real estate broker lien may *not* be filed in connection with which, if any, of the following transactions?

   a. The sale of a residential building containing five residential units.

   b. The sale of an office building.

   c. Both a and b.

   d. Neither a nor b.

10. In Pennsylvania, a power of attorney is

   a. presumed to be durable

   b. not presumed to be durable

   c. must be witnessed by two individuals who are 18 years of age or older

   d. both a and c

11. Under Pennsylvania law, which, if any, of the following statements is false?

   a. Any individual 18 years of age or older has the right to enter into contracts.

b. The age of majority is 18.

(c.) All contracts with minors are voidable.

d. None of the above are false.

12. Which, if any, of the following statements is (are) true?

a. Regarding the legal effect of a mortgage, Pennsylvania is an intermediate lien theory state.

b. In Pennsylvania, if a mortgagor defaults on his or her mortgage, the mortgagor does not automatically forfeit the property to the mortgagee.

(c.) Both a and b.

d. Neither a nor b.

13. After a foreclosure sale of residential property, many states, though not Pennsylvania, allow the property owner to pay off the amount due plus interest and costs pursuant to a right of

a. homeowner's priority

(b.) statutory redemption

c. homeowner's reversion

d. homeowners rescission

14. Pennsylvania real estate salespersons and brokers holding a standard license must complete a minimum of how many hours of Commission-approved continuing education within what period of time?

a. 30 hours every 3 years

(b.) 14 hours during the preceding license period

c. 28 hours during the preceding two license periods

d. both b and c are correct

15. Under Pennsylvania law, which of the following statements is false?

a. Although many states provide for some statutory period in which to redeem property after a foreclosure sale, Pennsylvania does not.

(b.) A purchaser of a timeshare or campground membership has the right to cancel the purchase until midnight of the seventh day following the date on which the purchaser executed the purchase contract.

c. The maximum that the Real Estate Recovery Fund will pay will not exceed $20,000 for anyone claim.

d. The maximum that the Real Estate Recovery Fund will pay will not exceed $100,000 per licensee.

16. Pennsylvania law

a. does not permit a broker to act as a dual agent

b. does not permit a broker to act as a single agent

c. does not permit a broker to act as a transaction licensee

(d) none of the above are true

17. In Pennsylvania, which, if any, of the following statements is (are) true?

a. A broker is permitted to act not as an agent who represents one or more parties to a real estate transaction, but to act as a mere middleman who brings the parties together and lets the parties do all of the negotiating among themselves.

b. A designated agent is a licensee designated by the employing broker, with the consent of the principal, to act exclusively as an agent on behalf of the principal to the exclusion of all other licensees within the broker's employ

(c) Both a and b are true.

d. Neither a nor b is true.

18. Evaluate the following two statements:

(i) In Pennsylvania, an exclusive listing may not contain an option by the broker to purchase the listed property.

(ii) In Pennsylvania, an exclusive listing may contain a listing period greater than six months.

a. The first statement is true; the second statement is false.

b. The first statement is false; the second statement is true

(c) The first statement is true; the second statement is true.

d. The first statement is false; the second statement is false

19. Under Pennsylvania law, which, if any, of the following statements is false?

a. At their first interview, licensees must provide individuals who wish to purchase residential property with a Consumer Notice.

b. At their first interview, licensees must provide individuals who wish to sell residential property with a Consumer Notice

c. At their first interview, licensees must provide individuals who wish to purchase commercial property with a Consumer Notice.

(d) None of the above statements in a-c is true.

20. Under Pennsylvania law, which if any of the following is (are) true?

a. A person employed by an owner of real estate for the purpose of managing or maintaining multifamily residential property need not be a real estate licensee.

b. An individual owner of real estate who leases his or her own real estate need not be a real estate licensee.

(c) Both a and b are true.

d. Neither a nor b is true.

21. Margaret is a broker who worked with Julie, a salesperson employed by broker Emily, who cooperated with Margaret in the sale of a condo.

a. Margaret may pay part of the commission she earned from this transaction to Julie.

b. Margaret may pay part of the commission she earned from this transaction to Emily.

c. Margaret may pay part of the commission she earned from this transaction to both Julie and Emily.

d. Margaret may pay part of the commission she earned from this transaction to neither Julie nor Emily.

22. George is a transaction licensee who is working with Susan to find her a home to purchase in a quiet, safe neighborhood. Which, if any, of the following statements is (are) true?

a. John does not need to have a valid salesperson or broker license.

b. John owes fiduciary duties to Susan.

c. Although John does not owe fiduciary duties to Susan, he is an agent for Susan.

d. None of the statements a-c is true.

23. Under Pennsylvania law, dual agency arises when

a. a broker represents two clients

b. a broker does not designate any affiliated licensees as designated agents

c. a broker who lists a property works with a cooperating broker who is the buyer's agent

d. none of the above

24. In Pennsylvania, individuals who apply for a salesperson license need not

a. be at least 18 years of age

b. have completed at least 60 hours in real estate instruction

c. be a resident of Pennsylvania.

d. have completed instruction that includes fair housing and professional ethics

25. A licensed Pennsylvania broker may deposit how much of the broker's own funds into an escrow account set up to hold client and customer funds?

a. Any amount to cover service charges to the account assessed by the banking institution

b. No more than $250.

c. No more than $100

d. $0

26. Kathy is the listing broker representing John, who wishes to sell his single-family house. Margaret is a broker cooperating with Kathy to find a buyer for John's house. Kathy has been feeling ill lately and wishes to reduce her workload.

  a. Kathy may delegate her agency relationship with John to Margaret.

  b. Kathy may compensate Margaret if a sale of John's house is completed.

  c. Both a and b are true

  d. Neither a nor b is true.

27. George is a Pennsylvania real estate salesperson who wishes to sell his own condo without listing the condo with a real estate company. George therefore creates and publishes an advertisement to sell his condo.

  a. George must disclose the name and telephone number of his employing broker in the advertisement.

  b. George must disclose in the advertisement that he is a real estate licensee.

  c. George does not need to disclose in the advertisement either that he is a licensee or the name and telephone number of his employing broker.

  d. Both a and b are true.

28. Any person who is found guilty of carrying on business activities restricted to a Pennsylvania real estate licensee without having a valid license may, after conviction of the third offense,

  a. be sentenced to pay a fine not exceeding $500 and/or to be imprisoned for not more than 3 months

  b. be sentenced to pay a fine not less than $1,000 but not more than $2,000 or to imprisonment for not less than one year but not more than two years, or both

  c. be sentenced to pay a fine not less than $2,000 but not more than $5,000 or to imprisonment for not less than one year but not more than two years, or both

  d. be sentenced to pay a fine not less than $500 but not more than $1,000 or to imprisonment for not less than one year but not more than two years, or both

29. When must a Pennsylvania licensee who represents the buyer of residential real estate give a prospective buyer the Consumer Notice?

  a. before or at the time the buyer signs an offer

  b. at the initial interview

  c. before or at the time the purchase agreement is signed by the buyer

  d. at closing

30. Which, if any, of the following agreements may be oral in Pennsylvania?

  a. an open listing agreement if the seller is provided with a written memorandum stating the terms of the agreement

60

b. a nonexclusive buyer agency agreement if the buyer is provided with a written memorandum stating the terms of the agreement

c. both a and b

d. neither a nor b

31. The economic characteristic of land that refers to the fact that the land and improvements to land are usually long-term investments, requiring large amounts of capital and long periods of time to recoup the investments, is referred to as

a. fixity or permanence of investment

b. indestructibility

c. scarcity

d. situs

32. Which of the following is not a governmental right?

a. adverse possession

b. zoning

c. taxation

d. eminent domain

33. The level of desire for a certain type of property refers to its

a. scarcity

b. demand

c. utility

d. transferability

34. Which of the following is false?

a. Private mortgage insurance (PMI) is insurance that lenders often require for loans with an LTV more than 80%.

b. PMI insurers the lender.

c. PMI covers the top amount of a loan in case of default.

d. The Homeowner's Protection Act applies to FHA-insured and VA-guaranteed loans.

35. Under a principle of agency law known as the _____, the authorization of an agent requires the same formality as is required for the act(s) the agent is hired to perform.

a. equal dignities rule

b. equal authorization rule

c. equal designation rule

d. equal formalities rule

36. The seller of a residential dwelling unit built before 1978 must

    a. pay for an inspection of the dwelling unit

    b. provide the buyer with an EPA pamphlet titled *How to Obtain a Home Warranty*

    c. offer the prospective buyer 5 days to inspect for lead-based paint and lead-based paint hazards

    d. offer the prospective buyer 10 days to inspect for lead-based paint and lead-based paint hazards

37. If I promise to pay you $20 if you mow my lawn on Tuesday, and you shrug your shoulders and say, "I'll see if I have the time," then unless I withdraw my offer in the meanwhile and you go ahead and mow my lawn on Tuesday

    a. I will owe you $20.

    b. I will not owe you $20 because you did not expressly accept my offer.

    c. I will not owe you $20 because there was never a "meeting of the minds."

    d. I will not owe you $20 because of the parol evidence rule.

38. A complete chronological history of all documents affecting the title to a property is

    a. a preliminary report

    b. a chain of title

    c. a title plant

    d. an opinion of title

39. The Federal Fair Housing Act

    a. prohibits refusal to loan in particular areas

    b. prohibits a private club, which, incident to its primary purpose, provides lodging for other than a commercial purpose, from limiting the rental or occupancy of such lodging to members

    c. limits the applicability of any reasonable local, State or Federal restrictions regarding the maximum number of occupants permitted to occupy a dwelling

    d. prohibits conduct against a person because such person has been convicted of the illegal manufacture or distribution of a controlled substance

40. Marcus has obtained a $323,000 loan to purchase a home for $380,000. What is the loan-to-value ratio of this transaction?

    a. 93%

    b. 80%

    c. 85%

    d. 84.2%

41. Under the Interstate Land Sales Full Disclosure Act, a developer must provide each prospective buyer with a Property Report that contains pertinent information about the subdivision and that discloses to the prospective buyer that he or she has a minimum of how many days in which to rescind the purchase agreement?

    a. 3

    b. 5

    c. 7

    d. 10

42. A township is how many miles square?

    a. 4

    b. 6

    c. 8

    d. 10

43. Master plans are required to address

    a. Transportation, housing, inverse condemnation

    b. Transportation, open spaces, noise

    c. Housing, conservation, deed restrictions

    d. Noise, open space, inverse condemnation

44. The value at which a lender is willing to make a loan on a property refers to the property's

    a. loan value

    b. assessed value

    c. appraised value

    d. insurance value

45. A fully amortized loan is

    a. a loan wherein the payments are sufficient to pay off the entire loan by the end of the loan term

    b. a loan wherein periodic payments consist of interest only

    c. a loan wherein the monthly payments pay all of the interest due but not enough of the principal to fully pay off the loan at the end of the loan term

    d. a loan wherein monthly installment payments do not cover all of the interest due

46. In states where the practice of designated agency is allowed,

a. the designated agent is a dual agent of the specified principal

b. the designated agent is an ostensible agent

c. disclosure of the designated agency relationship is required

d. the designated agent is a universal agent

47. A contract that is enforceable at the option of one party but not at the option of the other is

a. an unenforceable contract

b. a valid contract

c. a voidable contract

d. a void contract

48. Persons who receive property by way of intestate succession are referred to as

a. legatees

b. devisees

c. descentees

d. heirs

49. Over the years XYZ Bank has collected internal data conclusively demonstrating that residential loans made in areas of declining property values have a significantly greater default rate than loans secured by residential properties in other areas. XYZ Bank therefore has instituted a policy that it will no longer make loans of any kind secured by properties in areas where property values have been declining for three consecutive quarters. XYZ Bank's new policy is

a. legal because it is supported by good data

b. illegal blockbusting

c. illegal redlining

d. illegal steering

50. Anita is purchasing a house for $375,000 with 10% down. The lender requires 4.5 discount points. How much will Anita pay the lender for the discount points?

a. $13,500

b. $12,000

c. $15,187.50

d. $13,000

51. The term "boot" refers to

a. book value

b. actual depreciation

c. a 1099 exchange

d. a 1031 exchange

52. States where water is scarce typically adopt water rights based on

a. prior appropriation theory

b. riparian rights

c. littoral rights

d. the doctrine of capture

53. City and county zoning ordinances that require builders to set aside a given portion of new construction for people of low to moderate incomes are referred to as

a. nonconforming use

b. conditional use

c. spot zoning

d. inclusionary zoning

54. The maximum value of land is achieved when there is a reasonable degree of social, economic, and architectural conformity in the area is a statement of the principle of

a. progression

b. highest and best use

c. contribution

d. conformity

55. Interest rates on _____ loans vary over the term of the loan.

a. fully amortized

b. adjustable-rate

c. level payment

d. balloon

56. A real estate broker who represents both the seller and the buyer in a real estate transaction is

a. a subagent

b. an ostensible agent

c. a universal agent

d. a dual agent

57. Examples of "red flags" in real estate do not include

a. stains on ceilings or walls

b. potential purchasers with low FICO scores

c. warped floors or walls

d. the smell of mold

58. Persons not capable of contracting include

a. corporations

b. partnerships

c. neither a nor b

d. both a and b

59. A will written and signed by hand but not witnessed is

a. an invalid will

b. a nuncupative will

c. a holographic will

d. a formal will

60. Under the Equal Credit Opportunity Act, lenders may

a. ask if the applicant is divorced or widowed

b. ask if the applicant is married

c. ask about whether a woman of child-bearing age stop working

d. discount income based on sex or marital status

61. A home has a fair market value of $550,000, a homestead exemption of $100,000, an assessed value of $468,000, a county property tax of 1.2%, and a city property tax of .75%. What is the amount of city property tax savings due to the homestead exemption?

a. $3, 510

b. $7,176

c. $1,950

d. none of the above

62. A lien that is given by the owner of a property on which the lien is placed in order to use the property as security for debt is

a. an involuntary lien

b. a voluntary lien

c. a special assessment lien

d. a mechanics lien

63. A house has recently been built. The building inspector has discovered that the height of the house is 1½ feet greater than allowed by applicable zoning regulations. The owner of the house should apply for

   a. variance

   b. conditional use

   c. spot zoning

   d. nonconforming use

64. The economic life of a property

   a. determines the property's book value

   b. is referred to as its revitalization life expectancy

   c. almost always ends before its physical life ends

   d. almost always ends after its physical life ends

65. A balloon payment is

   a. a periodic payment consisting of interest only

   b. a payment, usually the final payment, of a loan that is significantly greater than prior payments

   c. a level interest payment

   d. a form of prepaid interest on a mortgage

66. An agency relationship is created by _____ in a situation where (1) an unauthorized person performs actions as if he or she were the agent of a principal, (2) the principal is aware of this conduct, and (3) the agent's actions and the principal's actions (or inactions) cause a third party to rely on the supposed agent's actions, believing that the actions are authorized by the principal.

   a. estoppel

   b. ratification

   c. express agreement

   d. the equal dignities rule

67. Consent to an agreement obtained by _____ is consent that may be _____.

   a. undue influence, freely given

   b. fraud, valid

   c. menace, rescinded

   d. duress, communicated by each to the other

68. A contract provision providing that if any term of the agreement is held to be ineffective or invalid, the remaining provisions will nevertheless be given full force and effect is

a. a severability clause

b. an ironclad merger clause

c. a contingency clause

d. a safety clause

69. Listing agreements in which a seller reserves the right to sell the property to a buyer procured by the seller without paying a commission to any broker are known as

a. exclusive agency listings

b. exclusive right to sell listing

c. open listings

d. both a and c

70. To be valid, a deed need not be

a. accepted by the grantee

b. delivered to the grantee

c. signed by the grantee

d. in writing

71. Broker Janet has noticed with concern that the property values in a section of town have been going down and crime rates have been going up ever since an influx of a particular minority group began three years ago. Eager to act in the best interests of her clients, Janet tells them that she would not show them homes in that section of town, and why. Janet's actions with her clients are

a. legal because she is fulfilling her fiduciary duty of care and loyalty to her clients

b. legal because her advice was based on verified statistics showing the correlation between the influx of the minority individuals and the increasing crime rate

c. illegal because her advice amounted to redlining

d. illegal because her advice amounted to blockbusting

72. Pursuant to the CAN-SPAM Act, the sender of a permissible email advertisement need not

a. tell recipients where the sender is located

b. honor a recipient's opt-out request within 5 business days

c. tell the recipients how to opt out of receiving future emails from the sender

d. identify the message as an ad

73. Marva is a real estate salesperson who found a buyer for a home that sold for $750,000. Marva's employing broker received a 5% commission for the sale. The agreement between the broker and Marva provides that she receive 40% of the broker's commission on every sale she procures. What is Marva's commission on this transaction?

a. $15,000

b. $18,750

c. $11,250

d. none of the above

74. The saying "first to record, first in right" refers to

a. actual notice

b. ad valorem taxation

c. lien priority

d. profit á prendre

75. The Comprehensive Environmental Response, Compensation, and Liability Act is also referred to as the

a. Remedial Action Law

b. Superfund Law

c. Removal Action Law

d. Responsible Party Law

76. The income approach to appraisal estimates the value of an income-producing property through which of the following three-step process?

a. determine the gross annual income, determine the appropriate depreciation rate, divide the net income by the capitalization rate

b. determine the net annual income, determine the appropriate capitalization rate, divide the net income by the capitalization rate

c. determine the net annual income, determine the appropriate depreciation rate, divide the gross income by the capitalization rate

d. determine the gross annual income, determine the appropriate capitalization rate, divide the gross income by the capitalization rate

77. Under an adjustable-rate loan, the interest rate remains fixed during certain time intervals referred to as the

a. adjustment periods

b. index periods

c. margin periods

d. carryover periods

78. Which of the following statements is false?

   a. A subagent is an agent of an agent.

   b. A single agent is an agent who represents only one party in a given transaction.

   c. A dual agent is an agent authorized by a real estate broker to represent a specific principal to the exclusion of all other agents in the brokerage.

   d. Ostensible agency is created when a principal intentionally, or by want of ordinary care, causes a third person to believe another to be his agent who is not actually employed by the principal.

79. State laws differ as to whether a seller of a single-family home must disclose that

   a. the roof leaks when it rains

   b. the prior owner was HIV-positive

   c. the seller is a Muslim

   d. the air conditioner doesn't work

80. A broker who has a listing agreement under which the broker is paid a set amount, not a percentage of the sale price, probably has which of the following listings?

   a. open listing

   b. exclusive right to sell listing

   c. exclusive agency listing

   d. flat fee listing

81. An option contract to purchase real estate

   a. must provide for a non-refundable option fee

   b. creates in the optionee the right of first refusal

   c. must contain all of the necessary terms of a real estate purchase agreement

   d. cannot provide for an option period greater than 1 year.

82. A deed is legally delivered to the grantee if

   a. the deed is physically delivered to the grantee and the grantor intends to pass title when the grantee eventually graduates from college.

   b. the deed is physically delivered to the grantee and the grantor intends that title passes after the grantor's death.

   c. the deed is physically delivered to the grantee.

   d. the deed is physically delivered to the grantee and the grantor intends that title immediately pass to the grantee.

83. Which of the following statements is true?

a. Under the Sherman Act, it is permissible for a broker to condition the sale of a property upon the broker's obtaining the listing for future sales.

b. Criminal penalties for price-fixing violations under the Sherman Act can be up to $1 million for an individual, along with 10 years in prison.

c. It would be legal for a state to pass a law requiring brokers not to discount their commissions below 2% of sales price.

d. It is not an antitrust violation for two competing brokers to agree not to do business with a broker whom they believe to be dishonest.

84. If $7,500 is loaned for one 30-day month on the basis of simple interest, and the total amount of interest due at the end of that month is $25, what annual rate of interest was charged if interest is calculated based on a 360 day year?

a. 4%

b. 3⅓ %

c. 4⅓ %

d. none of the above

85. Property tax liens

a. follow the "first to record, first in right" lien priority

b. are general taxes

c. are ad valorem taxes

d. are special assessments

86. A clear violation of an unambiguous condition in a private deed is likely to result in

a. monetary relief

b. injunctive relief

c. reversion of the title to the grantor

d. a court order requiring compliance with the condition

87. Loss in value due to general neighborhood deterioration is referred to as

a. economic obsolescence

b. functional obsolescence

c. deferred obsolescence

d. physical obsolescence

88. A loan based on the equity of a property is referred to as

a. a seller carry back loan

b. an equity loan

c. an installment loan

d. a level payment loan

89. Which of the following statements is false?

a. Agency by implication may be created if someone reasonably believes that someone else is acting as his or her agent, and the supposed agent corrects the impression.

b. By accepting or retaining the benefit of an act made by an unauthorized agent or by an agent who has exceeded his or her authority, a principal can create an agency by ratification.

c. There is a rule of equity known as estoppel that holds that one who causes another to rely on his or her words or actions shall be estopped (prohibited) from later taking a contrary position detrimental to the person who so relied.

d. Usually, an agency relationship is created by express agreement between the principal and the agent.

90. Categories of stigmatized properties include

a. properties that were once used as drug dens

b. properties located in floodplains

c. properties with leaky roofs

d. properties with defective air conditioners

91. The total amount of a commercial tenant's monthly lease payments is based in part on the tenant's gross receipts under a

a. triple net lease

b. percentage lease

c. graduated lease

d. gross lease

92. Constructive notice refers to

a. acknowledgment in front of an officer, such as a notary public

b. express transmission of information to the relevant party or parties

c. notice given to the public by the records available to the public

d. the delivery of a deed to the grantee

93. Joe and John, who are competing brokers, have lunch one day, during which they discuss how utterly dishonest broker Bob is. After this lunch meeting, Joe refuses to discuss business with Bob, but John continues to do business with Bob as usual.

a. Joe but not John could be guilty of group boycott.

b. John but not Joe could be guilty of group boycott.

c. Both John and Joe could be guilty of group boycott.

d. Neither John nor Joe is likely to have violated the prohibition against group boycott.

94. Homes comparable to Natalie's in the area have an average monthly gross rent multiplier of 280. The fair market value of Natalie's home is $1,743,000. Using the gross rent multiplier approach, what monthly rent should Natalie get for renting her home?

a. $6,225

b. $8,715

c. $6,214 (rounded)

d. none of the above

95. A monetary encumbrance on property as security for a debt or obligation is

a. an express grant

b. a lien

c. an easement

d. a prescription

96. Using police power, governments have the right to create

a. deed restrictions

b. inverse condemnation

c. zoning codes

d. covenants and conditions

97. Primary factors for which adjustments in comparable properties must be made in a CMA include all of the following except

a. number of bedrooms

b. age of the owner

c. financing

d. property rights

98. A subprime loan is a

a. loan that carries an interest rate below the current prime rate of interest

b. conforming loan

c. loan made to a borrower who has a relatively high-risk profile

d. loan made to a borrower who has a relatively low-risk profile

99. Which of the following statements is true?

a. A dual agent owes fiduciary duties to the seller but not to the buyer.

b. All real estate agency compensation is subject to negotiation.

c. The source of compensation determines agency representation.

d. In a few states, an agent's compensation is fixed by custom.

100. Alex and Sarah sign a written purchase agreement in which Alex agrees to purchase Sara's condo for a specified price sometime within the next six months. Their agreement is

a. bilateral, implied, and executory

b. unilateral, executed, and enforceable

c. bilateral, executory, and express

d. express, executory, and avoidable

101. Under _____, the lender merely gives the debtor proper notice and prepares the proper papers; a court sets a period of time for the debtor to redeem the property by paying all past-due payments; and if the debtor fails to so redeem the property, title passes to the lender and the debtor loses all rights and interests (including equity) in the property.

a. nonjudicial foreclosure

b. judicial foreclosure

c. strict foreclosure

d. one-action foreclosure

102. In the middle of the winter with the temperature hovering near zero, agent Bob, having been informed by a home inspector that the air conditioner in the house Bob is showing has a defective air-conditioner, tells a prospective customer that all the amenities of the house are in perfect condition. If this customer purchases the house, agent Bob probably would best be protected by

a. having E & O insurance

b. voluntarily relinquishing his license

c. hiring a good lawyer

d. moving to another state

103. Examples of non-freehold estates include

a. life estates

b. leases

c. fee simple estates

d. fee simple defeasible estates

104. One of the reasons why VA-guaranteed loans are attractive does not include

a. the loans do not require a down payment

b. underwriting standards are less stringent than for FHA or conventional loans

c. no mortgage insurance required

d. the loans are not assumable

105. Conversion is

a. the act of placing funds belonging to clients or customers into accounts also holding the agent's funds

b. the process of ascertaining value by comparing and evaluating values obtained from comparables or from different valuation approaches

c. the act of creating an agency relationship by a principal who accepts or retains the benefit of an act made by an unauthorized agent

d. the unauthorized use of another's funds for one's own use

106. When the purpose of the agent's job is accomplished,

a. the agency is terminated by a change in law

b. the agency is terminated by being coupled with an interest

c. the agency is terminated because of substantial misrepresentation

d. the agency is terminated

107. Lucy signed an exclusive right to sell listing with Broker Joe. Joe procures a buyer ready, willing, and able to meet Lucy's terms as stated in a listing agreement. Which of the following statements is true?

a. Lucy and the buyer have a binding purchase agreement.

b. If Lucy refuses to sell, Joe can probably obtain specific performance.

c. Lucy must accept the buyer's offer and the pay Joe the agreed-upon consideration

d. Lucy does not need to accept the buyer's offer, but she owes Joe the agreed-upon commission.

108. For 25% of the loot, Hank agreed with Joe to drive the getaway car during the robbery Joe planned. Hank and Joe have

a. a voidable contract

b. a void contract

c. an executed contract

d. a valid, bilateral contract

109. John is a widower who lives in a rather large home the couple purchased 40 years ago. Wanting some company in his old age, and a little extra income, John decides to rent the maid's room. While interviewing prospective renters, John makes it known that he only wants to rent to a white Christian woman over the age of 50.

a. John is doing nothing illegal because his is an owner-occupied, single-family home, which is exempt from Federal Fair Housing Act rules.

b. John is violating Federal Fair Housing Act rules that protect against religious discrimination in housing.

c. John is violating Federal Fair Housing Act rules that protect against sex and age discrimination in housing.

d. John is violating the Civil Rights Act of 1866.

110. Olivia tells her listing agent that she wants to convey title by way of the type of deed that will give her the greatest protection. Her listing agent should inform her that the deed she is looking for is a

a. quitclaim deed

b. grant deed

c. special warranty deed

d. general warranty deed

ANSWERS TO PRACTICE EXAM #1:

Note: If you would like to obtain a deeper understanding of the real estate principles behind the answers to the **national** portion of the exam, please consult the supplemental textbook *PSI Real Estate Exam Prep 2015-2016*, which provides a thorough, up-to-date review of the real estate principles covered in the **national** portion of the Pennsylvania real estate exam. This textbook is available both in print and Kindle formats on Amazon.com.

1.   **d.** Section 8(i) of the Seller Property Disclosure Statement asks "What is the source of your drinking water?"

2.   **c.** Pennsylvania uses the metes and bounds and the lot and block descriptions but not the rectangular survey description.

3.   **b.** Pennsylvania has adopted the two common law categories of fee simple defeasible estates: fee simple determinable and fee simple subject to a condition subsequent. A fee simple determinable is an estate that automatically reverts to the grantor upon the occurrence of a specified event with no need to take court action. A fee simple subject to a condition subsequent is an estate that, upon the noncompliance of the stated condition, the grantor or the grantor's successors in interest would have the right to terminate the preceding estate but must take court action to assert the right of termination and reversion. "While" is considered a special limiting word used to convey a fee simple determinable.

4.   **c.** Under Pennsylvania law, a conventional life estate is created by a grantor granting a life interest to someone, either based on the grantee's life or on a third person's life (a life estate pur autre vie). A legal life estate (also referred to as a statutory life estate) is created by operation of the Pennsylvania probate, Estates, and Fiduciaries Code.

5.   **b.** Although Martha has been doing this for the 21 years required by Pennsylvania law to acquire a prescriptive easement, the use has not been "continuous."

6.   **b.** Pennsylvania Landlord and Tenant Act §250.501(b) states that for a (non-mobile home) lease with a term of one year or less, if 15-day notice is required.

7.   **d.** Under Pennsylvania law, a conveyance of real property to a husband and wife is presumed to create a tenancy by the entireties.

8.   **a.** Pennsylvania Mechanics' Lien Law states that to perfect a lien, every claimant must file a claim with the prothonotary of the court or court of common pleas of the county in which the improvement is situate within 6 months after completion of his work.

9.   **d.** The Pennsylvania Commercial Real Estate Broker Lien Act provides that "commercial real estate" under the Act does not include real estate containing 1 to 4 residential units and certain real estate zoned for agricultural purposes, but does include other commercial real estate. *Note: be careful with questions that contain the word "not."*

10.   **d.** Chapter 56 of the Pennsylvania Consolidated Statutes provides that a power of attorney is presumed to be durable and must be witnessed by *two* individuals, each of whom is 18 years of age or older.

11.   **c.** Common law in Pennsylvania holds that contracts with minors for "necessaries" are not voidable.

12.   **c.** Although Pennsylvania traditionally was a title theory state, it has adopted intermediate lien theory, which means that before a mortgagee can acquire possession of defaulted property, the mortgagee must give proper notice of default to the mortgagor and

provide the mortgagor the opportunity to cure the default before proceeding with foreclosure.

13. **b.** Although many states provide for some statutory period in which to redeem property after a foreclosure sale, Pennsylvania does not.

14. **b.** Section 35.382(a) of Pennsylvania's Rules and Regulations of the State Real Estate Commission provides that 14 hours of Commission-approved continuing education must be completed during the preceding license period. Completing 28 hours during one license period would not help satisfy the continuing education requirement for the following license period.

15. **b.** Section 455.609(a) provides that a purchaser of a timeshare or campground membership shall have the right to cancel the purchase until midnight of the *fifth* day following the date on which the purchaser executed the purchase contract.

16. **d.** A Pennsylvania real estate broker *may* act in any of the capacities stated in a-c.

17. **c.** Pennsylvania law provides for transaction licensee status, under which a licensee does not act as an agent of either party and does not owe a fiduciary duty to either party. *See,* §455.201 of Pennsylvania's Real Estate Licensing and Registration Act (RELRA). Section 455.201 also provides for designated agency as stated in b.

18. **c.** Section 35.32 (c) of Pennsylvania's Rules and Regulations of the State Real Estate Commission states that both statements are correct. An exclusive listing may contain a listing period exceeding six months, but not exceeding one year.

19. **d.** Section 35.284 of Pennsylvania's Rules and Regulations of the State Real Estate Commission provides that all consumers seeking to sell or purchase residential property must be given a Consumer Notice, and that all *individuals* (i.e., natural persons) seeking to sell or purchase commercial property must be given a Consumer Notice. Therefore, the only statement in choices a-d that is false is choice d because choice d asserts that none of the choices a-c is true when, in fact, all of the choices a-c are true.

20. **c.** Pursuant to section 455.304 of Pennsylvania's Real Estate Licensing and Regulation Act, an exception to licensing requirements applies to any person employed by an owner of real estate for the purpose of managing or maintaining multifamily residential property: provided, however, that such person is not authorized or empowered by such owner to enter into leases on behalf of the owner, to negotiate terms or conditions of occupancy with current or prospective tenants or to hold money belonging to tenants other than on behalf of the owner. So long as the owner retains the authority to make all such decisions, the employees may show apartments and provide information on rental amounts, building rules and regulations and leasing determinations. Additionally, an owner of real estate who leases his or her own real estate need not be a real estate licensee. In the case of a partnership or corporation, this exclusion shall not extend to more than five of its partners or officers, respectively, nor to other partnership or corporation personnel or employees.

21. **b.** Section 455.604(12.1) of Pennsylvania's Real Estate Licensing and Registration Act (RELRA) states that the paying of a commission or any valuable consideration by a broker to anyone other than his or her licensed employees or another real estate broker for any act requiring a real estate license is prohibited.

22. **d.** Pennsylvania law provides for transaction licensee status, under which a licensee must be a licensed salesperson or broker but does *not* act as an agent of either party and does not owe a fiduciary duty to either party. *See,* §455.201 of Pennsylvania's Real Estate Licensing and Registration Act (RELRA).

23. **d.** Choice a does not create dual agency unless the two clients happen to be the seller

and the buyer in the same transaction. Choice b does not create a dual agency in the broker unless one of the broker's affiliated licensees represents the seller and a second affiliated licensee represents the buyer in the same transaction. Choice c does not create a dual agency because a broker does not necessarily represent a cooperating broker's client.

24.   **c.** One does not need to be a resident of Pennsylvania to acquire a salesperson license.

25.   **a.** Pursuant to RELRA §455.68e(j), a broker is permitted to deposit the broker's own funds into an escrow account in an amount to cover service charges to the account assessed by the banking institution.

26.   **b.** Although a broker may compensate a cooperating broker, a broker may not extend or delegate the broker's agency relationship with a principal to another broker without the written consent of the principal. *See*, RELRA §455.606a(c).

27.   **b.** Pursuant to Pennsylvania Rules and Regulations of the Real Estate Commission §304, a licensee who sells or leases his own real estate shall disclose that he is a real estate licensee in advertisements for the property. This requirement does not apply if the property is listed with a real estate company.

28.   **c.** Pursuant to RELRA §455.303, any person who is found guilty of carrying on business activities restricted to a Pennsylvania real estate licensee without having a valid license may, after conviction of *a second or subsequent offense*, be sentenced to pay a fine not less than $2,000 but not more than $5,000 or to imprisonment for not less than one year but not more than two years, or both.

29.   **b.** Pursuant to Pennsylvania Rules and Regulations of the Real Estate Commission §336(a) for the purchase or sale of residential or commercial real estate or for the lease of residential or commercial real estate when the licensee is working on behalf of the tenant, licensees shall provide the consumer with the Consumer Notice at their initial interview.

30.   **c.** Pursuant to Pennsylvania Rules and Regulations of the State Real Estate Commission §35.281(b)1), open listing agreements or nonexclusive buyer agency agreements may be oral if the seller/buyer or landlord/tenant is provided with a written memorandum stating the terms of the agreement.

31.   **a.** The economic characteristic of land that refers to the fact that the land and improvements to land are usually long-term investments, requiring large amounts of capital and long periods of time to recoup the investments, is referred to as fixity or permanence of investment.

32.   **a.** The government cannot acquire property by adverse possession.

33.   **b.** Demand refers to the level of desire for a property.

34.   **d.** The Homeowner's Protection Act does not apply to FHA-insured and VA-guaranteed loans.

35.   **a.** Under a principle of agency law known as the equal dignities rule, the authorization of an agent requires the same formality as is required for the act(s) the agent is hired to perform.

36.   **d.** The seller must offer a prospective buyer 10 days to inspect for lead-based paint and lead-based paint hazards. The seller is not required to pay for this inspection.

37.   **a.** Your act of mowing my lawn constituted both your acceptance of my offer and your full performance.

38.   **b.** A chain of title is a complete chronological history of all documents affecting the title to a property.

39.   **a.** The Federal Fair Housing Act prohibits refusal to loan in particular areas.

40.   **c.** $\$323,000 \div \$380,000 = .85 = 85\%$.

41.   **c.** Under the Interstate Land Sales Full Disclosure Act, a developer must provide each prospective buyer with a Property Report that contains pertinent information about the subdivision and that discloses to the prospective buyer that he or she has a minimum of 7 days in which to rescind the purchase agreement.

42.   **b.** A township is a six mile square parcel of land consisting of 36 sections.

43.   **b.** Master plans are required to address transportation, housing, conservation, open spaces, noise, and safety.

44.   **a.** Loan value (also referred to as mortgage value) is the value at which a lender is willing to make a loan on the property.

45.   **a.** A fully amortized loan is a loan wherein the payments are sufficient to pay off the entire loan by the end of the loan term.

46.   **c.** In states where the practice of designated agency is allowed, disclosure of the designated agency relationship is required.

47.   **c.** A voidable contract is a contract that is enforceable at the option of one party but not at the option of the other, as when the consent of one party (the party who may elect to have the contract enforced) is obtained by fraud (not forgery, which would render the contract void), coercion, misrepresentation, or undue influence.

48.   **d.** Persons who receive property by way of intestate succession are referred to as heirs.

49.   **c.** The Federal Fair Housing Act prohibits the practice of refusing to loan in particular areas — a practice known as redlining.

50.   **c.** The loan amount is $\$375,000 - \$37,500$ (the down payment) $= \$337,500$. $\$337,500 \times .045 = \$15,187.50$.

51.   **d.** If a 1031 exchange has been properly structured, neither gain nor loss is recognized at the time of the exchange. If, on the other hand, a like-kind property is received in exchange along with boot (cash or other not like-kind property), gain is recognized on the value of the boot at the time of the exchange, but losses are still excluded from recognition at the time of the exchange.

52.   **a.** States where water is scarce typically adopt water rights based on prior appropriation theory.

53.   **d.** Inclusionary zoning refers to city and county zoning ordinances that require builders to set aside a given portion of new construction for people of low to moderate incomes.

54.   **d.** The principle of conformity states that the maximum value of land is achieved when there is a reasonable degree of social, economic, and architectural conformity in the area. For a particular property, however, nonconformity may benefit or reduce the property's value.

55.   **b.** Interest rates on adjustable-rate loans vary over the term of the loan.

56.   **d.** A real estate broker who represents both the seller and the buyer in a real estate transaction is a dual agent.

57.   **b.** A red flag is a condition that should alert a reasonably attentive person of a potential problem with the condition of a property that warrants further investigation. Examples include stains on ceilings or walls, the smell of mold, and warped floors or walls.

58.   **c.** Both corporations and partnerships are capable of contracting. Be careful to read questions and answers carefully, especially those with the word "not" in them.

59.   **c.** A will written and signed by hand but not witnessed is a holographic will.

60.   **b.** Under the ECOA, a lender may ask if the applicant is married, unmarried (meaning single, divorced, or widowed), or separated, but may not ask if the applicant is divorced or widowed.

61.   **d.** $100,000 × .0075 = $750.

62.   **b.** A voluntary lien is a lien voluntarily given by the owner of the land upon which the lien is placed, usually to secure repayment of long-term debt.

63.   **a.** Variance refers to an exception that may be granted in cases where damage to the value of a property from the strict enforcement of zoning ordinances would far outweigh any benefit to be derived from enforcement.

64.   **c.** The economic life of a property almost always ends before its physical life ends.

65.   **b.** A balloon payment is a payment, usually the final payment, of a loan that is significantly greater than prior payments.

66.   **a.** An agency relationship is created by estoppel in a situation where (1) an unauthorized person performs actions as if he or she were the agent of a principal, (2) the principal is aware of this conduct, and (3) the agent's actions and the principal's actions (or inactions) cause a third party to rely on the supposed agent's actions, believing that the actions are authorized by the principal.

67.   **c.** Consent that is not freely given, such as consent obtained by duress, menace, fraud, or undue influence, is consent that may be rescinded.

68.   **a.** A severability clause is a contract provision providing that if any term of the agreement is held to be ineffective or invalid, the remaining provisions will nevertheless be given full force and effect.

69.   **d.** In both an open listing and in an exclusive agency listing the seller reserves the right to sell the property to a buyer procured by the seller, without paying any commission to a broker.

70.   **c.** Although to be valid, a deed must be signed by the grantor, it need not be signed by the grantee.

71.   **d.** Fulfilling what she honestly thought was her fiduciary duty to her clients is not a defense against the FFHA's prohibition of blockbusting.

72.   **b.** Any opt-out mechanism offered must be able to process opt-out requests for at least 30 days after sending the email, and any opt-out request must be honored within 10 business days.

73.   **a.** The broker's commission is 5% of $750,000 = $37,500. Therefore, Marva's commission is 40% of $37,500 = $15,000.

74.   **c.** The saying "first to record, first in right" refers to lien priority.

75.   **b.** The Comprehensive Environmental Response, Compensation, and Liability Act is also referred to as the Superfund Law.

76.   **b.** The income approach estimates the value of an income-producing property as being an investment (like stocks or bonds) worth the present value of the future income of the property through a three-step process: (1) determine the net annual income, (2) determine an appropriate capitalization rate, and (3) divide the net income by the capitalization rate to obtain the estimate of value; i.e., value = net income ÷ capitalization rate.

77.   **a.** Under an adjustable-rate loan, the interest rate remains fixed during certain time intervals referred to as the adjustment periods.

78.   **c.** A dual agent is a real estate broker who represents both the seller and the buyer in a real estate transaction.

79.   **b.** Some states have exempted certain facts — such as long-ago deaths on the property or the property having been inhabited by a resident who committed suicide or who had AIDS or is HIV-positive — from required disclosures.

80.   **d.** A flat fee listing is a listing in which the broker's compensation is a set amount rather than a percentage of the sale price.

81.   **c.** Because when an option is exercised it becomes a purchase agreement, an option contract to purchase real estate must contain all of the necessary terms of such a purchase. Additionally, though an optionee must give sufficient consideration to acquire an option, the option fee can be refundable, because there would still be consideration consisting of the optionee's being unable to use the money in the meanwhile, and the optionor's being able to use the money in the meanwhile.

82.   **d.** A deed is not effective until it is legally delivered to the grantee. Delivery of a deed in this context is a legal, not a physical, concept. Actual physical delivery is not sufficient; there must be an unconditional intent on the part of the grantor to pass title *immediately* to the grantee.

83.   **b.** The Sherman Act provides for both civil and criminal penalties, both of which can be severe. Criminal penalties can be up to $100 million for a corporation and up to $1 million for an individual, along with up to 10 years in prison.

84.   **a.** $25 (interest) = $7,500 × Annual Interest Rate ÷ 12.
Therefore, annual interest rate = ($25 ÷ $7,500) × 12 = .04 = 4%.

85.   **c.** General real estate taxes are ad valorem taxes.

86.   **c.** A clear violation of an unambiguous condition in a private deed is likely to result in reversion of the title to the grantor.

87.   **a.** Loss in value due to general neighborhood deterioration is referred to as economic or external obsolescence.

88.   **b.** A loan based on the equity of a property is referred to as an equity loan.

89.   **a.** Agency by implication may be created if someone reasonably believes that someone else is acting as his or her agent, and the supposed agent *fails to correct* the impression.

90.   **a.** A stigmatized property is a property having a condition that certain persons may find materially negative in a way that does not relate to the property's actual physical condition.

91.   **b.** Under a percentage lease, which is often used in shopping centers, the tenant typically pays a base rent amount plus a percentage of the gross receipts of the tenant's business.

92. **c.** Constructive notice (as distinct from actual notice, which is express notice of information given in fact) refers to notice given to the public by the records available to the public.

93. **d.** A group boycott occurs when two or more brokers agree, explicitly or implicitly, not to deal with another broker or brokers. Here, Joe and John did not agree to boycott Bob, nor did they subsequently act in unison to boycott Bob.

94. **a.** $1,743,000 ÷ 280 = $6,225.

95. **b.** A lien is an official charge against property as security for the payment of a debt or an obligation owed for services rendered.

96. **c.** Police power, which is the power of government to impose restrictions on private rights, including property rights, includes building codes, zoning codes, subdivision regulations, and property setbacks.

97. **b.** Primary factors for which adjustments in comparable properties must be made in a CMA include property rights, financing, and number of bedrooms.

98. **c.** A subprime loan is a loan made to a borrower who has a relatively high-risk profile.

99. **b.** All real estate compensation is subject to negotiation — it is not fixed by law or custom.

100. **c.** The contract is bilateral because Alex's promise to purchase was exchanged for Sara's promise to sell; executory because neither side has yet completed performance; and express because it is in writing.

101. **c.** In a strict foreclosure, the lender merely gives the debtor proper notice and prepares the proper papers; a court sets a period of time for the debtor to redeem the property by paying all past-due payments; and if the debtor fails to so redeem the property, title passes to the lender and the debtor loses all rights and interests (including equity) in the property.

102. **c.** E & O insurance does not cover acts of fraud.

103. **b.** Leasehold estates are non-freehold estates.

104. **d.** VA-guaranteed loans *are* assumable if approved by the VA.

105. **d.** Conversion is the unauthorized use of another's funds for one's own use.

106. **d.** When the purpose of the agent's job is accomplished — such as by the sale of a property if the agent is a listing agent, or the purchase of a property if the agent is a buyer's agent — the agency ends.

107. **d.** Because a listing agreement is not an offer to sell, it cannot be accepted by a buyer. However, the broker fully performed his part of the listing agreement, so is due his full commission.

108. **b.** The illegal object of this contract makes it void.

109. **d.** The Civil Rights Act of 1866 prohibits *all* racial discrimination in the lease or sale of real and personal property. The fact that John's property is exempt from the FFHA does not mean that his property is exempt from all other applicable antidiscrimination laws.

110. **a.** A quitclaim deed conveys no warranties of any kind, which therefore would present Olivia with the fewest risks of any type of deed that she can voluntarily give.

PRACTICE EXAM #2:

Note: Questions 1-30 of this exam consist of *state-portion* questions of the Pennsylvania real estate exam. Questions 31-110 of this exam consist of *national-portion* questions of the Pennsylvania relics eight exam.

1. The Pennsylvania Coal Severance Notice is concerned with

    a. mine subsidence

    b. profit á prendre

    c. displacement by appurtenance

    d. lis pendens support

2. Pennsylvania uses which of the following methods of legal land description?

    a. rectangular survey system

    b. government survey system

    c. both a and b

    d. Neither a nor b

3. Bob conveys a vacant lot to Joe "so long as" the property is not used to sell alcohol. Joe receives a

    a. fee simple absolute

    b. fee simple determinable

    c. fee simple subject to a condition subsequent

    d. life estate

4. Under Pennsylvania law, a surviving spouse is entitled to a life estate equal to how much the value of the deceased spouse's estate if the deceased spouse wills all of his or her estate to another?

    a. none

    b. one third

    c. one half

    d. 100%

5. Martha, who owns a home next to Emily's property, has, without Emily's approval, walked across Emily's backyard on a well-worn path every day for the past 15 years. Joe, from whom Martha purchased her home, had also walked across Emily's property without Emily's approval on the same path every day for the 10 years immediately prior to selling his house to Martha.

    a. Martha has a prescriptive easement.

b. Martha does not have a prescriptive easement.

c. Martha has a license to use.

d. Martha has acquired a path by attachment.

6. Ruth has a month-to-month lease for Bob's condo. Ruth is delinquent on her rent payment, and Bob has sent her a demand for payment to which she has not responded. Bob now wishes to give Ruth notice to quit, giving her the least amount of time acceptable under Pennsylvania law. Bob should give Ruth a

a. one-month notice

b. 10-day notice

c. notice to quit immediately

d. 15-day notice

7. Pennsylvania recognizes three discrete, severable estates in land: the surface estate, the mineral estate, and the

a. easement estate

b. appurtenance estate

c. coal estate

d. right to subjacent support

8. Under Pennsylvania law, what is the minimum notice that tenants of an apartment building being converted into a condominium must be given before such tenants are required to vacate?

a. One month

b. Two months

c. Six months

d. One year

9. Margaret purchases a new sofa on credit for her Pennsylvania home. The sofa costs $501. The credit contract contains conspicuous confession of judgment clauses, which Margaret reads and signs. This confession of judgment likely is

a. enforceable because the amount of credit exceeds $500

b. enforceable because the amount of credit did not exceed $10,000

c. enforceable because the sofa was for Margaret's own personal use

d. not enforceable

10. In Pennsylvania, a power of attorney is

a. presumed to be durable

b. presumed not to be durable

85

c. must be witnessed by one individual who is 18 years of age or older

d. both a and c

11. Which of the following statements is false under Pennsylvania law?

a. A person must be 18 years of age or older to make a will.

b. A person must be of sound mind to make a will.

c. Legally adopted children are considered heirs of their adopting parents.

d. All wills must be witnessed.

12. Under Pennsylvania's Electronic Transactions Act, which of the following statements is false?

a. The Act does not require for its application that the parties to a transaction must agree to conduct the transaction by electronic means.

b. The Act provides that a record or instrument may not be denied legal effect solely because it is in electronic form.

c. The Act provides that a contract not be denied legal effect because an electronic record was used.

d. If a law requires a record to be in writing, an electronic record satisfies the law.

13. Under Pennsylvania law, which of the following statements is false?

a. A homeowner in default on his or her mortgage may reinstate the mortgage up to one hour before a foreclosure sale.

b. A homeowner whose home was foreclosed on has a statutory right of redemption after the foreclosure sale.

c. A party foreclosing on residential property must give the borrower a notice of intention to foreclose and an opportunity to cure the default at least 30 days before beginning the foreclosure.

d. A party foreclosing on residential property must give the borrower a notice that the borrower may qualify for financial assistance under Pennsylvania's Homeowner's Emergency Mortgage Assistance Program (HEMAP) at least 30 days before foreclosing.

14. Emily and Roberta are partners who own a 20-unit apartment building in Pennsylvania. Roberta does all of the advertising for, and all of the negotiating and signing of, leases for their apartments, while Emily collects the rent, takes care of the books, and handles all of the maintenance.

a. Roberta, but not Emily, must obtain a real estate license.

b. Emily, but not Roberta, must obtain a real estate license.

c. Neither Emily nor Roberta needs to obtain a real estate license with respect to the work they do on their apartment building.

d. Both Roberta and Emily must obtain a real estate license.

15. Which of the following statements is (are) true?

a. A broker's comparative market analysis must be performed in accordance with the Uniform Standards of Professional Appraisal Practice.

b. At the initial interview between a licensee and a prospective seller, the licensee must disclose, among other things, that the broker's fees are negotiable.

c. Both a and b

d. Neither a nor b

16. Pursuant to Pennsylvania law, which of the following statements is false?

a. A licensee may not participate in a real estate transaction involving property in which the licensee has an ownership interest unless the licensee first discloses the licensee's interest in writing to all parties concerned.

b. A licensee may not represent, or purport to represent, more than one party to a real estate transaction without the written consent of all parties concerned.

c. A broker who manages rental property may not accept a commission, rebate or profit on expenditures made for the lessor without the lessor's written consent.

d. A licensee who sells his or her *own* real estate, does not need to inform the purchaser that the licensee is a real estate licensee.

17. In Pennsylvania,

a. all real estate listing agreements must be in writing.

b. a broker's comparative market analysis must be performed in accordance with the Uniform Standards of Professional Appraisal Practice.

c. both a and b are true.

d. neither a nor b is true.

18. In Pennsylvania, an exclusive listing may not contain

a. a cancellation notice to terminate the agreement at the end of the listing period set forth in the agreement

b. an option by the broker to purchase the listed property

c. both a and b are true

d. neither a nor b is true

19. Under Pennsylvania law, which, if any, of the following statements is true?

a. The fact that a structural element, system or subsystem is *near* the end of its normal useful life is not by itself a material defect.

b. The fact that a structural element, system or subsystem is *beyond* the end of its normal useful life is not by itself a material defect.

c. Both a and b are true.

d. Neither a nor b is true.

20. In Pennsylvania, when must each party to a real estate sale be provided with a written estimate of reasonably foreseeable expenses associated with the sale that the party may be expected to pay?

    a. Before the agreement of sale is executed.

    b. At or before the time the listing agreement is signed.

    c. At or before the offer to purchase is signed.

    d. Before escrow is opened.

21. John is an associate broker employed by broker José. John has worked with José and with José's cooperating broker, Manuel, to make a sale of a single-family home. John may not accept a commission or other valuable consideration for his work in this transaction from

    a. the seller of the home

    b. the buyer of the home

    c. Manuel

    d. all of the above

22. Sandra is a transaction licensee who is working with a seller of a condo. Which, if any, of the following statements is (are) true?

    a. Sandra owes fiduciary duties to the seller.

    b. Sandra does not need to have a valid salesperson or broker license.

    c. Sandra must act fairly, honestly and competently to find qualified buyers of the seller's condo.

    d. None of the statements a-c is true.

23. Broker Kathy designated her affiliated licensees, Joe and Ted, to represent the seller and buyer, respectively, in a real estate transaction involving the sale of a home. Under Pennsylvania law

    a. Kathy is a dual agent

    b. Joe and Ted are both dual agents

    c. both a and b are true statements

    d. neither a nor b is a true statement

24. In Pennsylvania, which, if any, of the following does (do) not need to have a license or registration certificate?

    a. Building-owner salesperson.

    b. Rental listing referral agent.

    c. Cemetery salesperson.

    d. Each of the above must have a license or registration certificate.

25. In Pennsylvania, an individual who applies for a cemetery broker's license need not

    a. be 21 years of age or older

    b. have completed at least 240 hours of Commission-approved education

    c. take and pass a cemetery broker's license exam

    d. have been engaged full time as a salesperson or cemetery salesperson for at least three years or possess educational or experience qualifications which the commission deems to be the equivalent thereof

26. Joan is a licensee representing Lynn, the owner of a condo. Mike is a potential buyer whom Joan does not represent.

    a. Joan owes fiduciary duties to Mike.

    b. Joan must disclose to Mike any conflict of interest.

    c. Joan does not need to deal with Mike honestly and fairly because Mike is not her client.

    d. Joan does not need to advise Mike to seek expert advice on matters relating to the transaction that are beyond Joan's expertise because Mike is not her client.

27. An advertisement by an associate broker or salesperson *must* contain

    a. the business name of the employing broker

    b. the telephone number of the employing broker

    c. both a and b

    d. neither a nor b

28. Any person who is found guilty of carrying on business activities restricted to a Pennsylvania real estate licensee without having a valid license may, after conviction of the second offense,

    a. be sentenced to pay a fine not exceeding $500 and/or to be imprisoned for not more than 3 months

    b. be sentenced to pay a fine not less than $2,000 but not more than $5,000 or to imprisonment for not less than one year but not more than two years, or both

    c. be sentenced to pay a fine not less than $1,000 but not more than $2,000 or to imprisonment for not less than one year but not more than two years, or both

    d. be sentenced to pay a fine not less than $500 but not more than $1,000 or to imprisonment for not less than one year but not more than two years, or both

29. Evaluate the following two statements according to Pennsylvania law:

(i) A broker must preserve records relating to a real estate transaction for at least five years after consummation of the transaction.

(ii) A real estate license may be placed on inactive status for no more than three years.

    a. The first statement is true and the second statement is true.

b. The first statement is true and the second statement is false.

c. The first statement is false and the second statement is false.

d. The first statement is false and the second statement is true

30. Which of the following agreements may be oral in Pennsylvania?

a. an open listing agreement if the seller is provided with a written memorandum stating the terms of the agreement

b. an exclusive agency listing agreement if the seller is provided with a written memorandum stating the terms of the agreement

c. an exclusive buyer agency agreement if the buyer is provided with a written memorandum stating the terms of the agreement

d. an exclusive right to sell listing agreement if the seller is provided with a written memorandum stating the terms of the agreement

31. Tests used by courts to determine whether an item is a fixture include

a. adaptability of the attached item, method of severability, intent of the person attaching the item

b. relationship of the parties, how long the item has been on the property, adaptability of the attached item

c. how long the item has been on the property, intent of the person attaching the item, agreement between the parties

d. agreement between the parties, adaptability of the attached item, relationship of the parties

32. The due process proceeding for eminent domain actions is called

a. severance

b. assessment

c. condemnation

d. ad valorem

33. The lack of abundance of a certain type of property refers to its

a. utility

b. transferability

c. scarcity

d. market value

34. Which of the following statements is false?

a. Discount points are sometimes referred to as loan equalization factors.

b. Discount points can be a form of prepaid interest.

c. A discount point is equal to 1% of the purchase price.

d. LTV is an important risk factor that lenders use to assess the viability of a proposed loan.

35. A _____ agent is an agent given power of attorney to act on behalf of a principal for an unlimited range of legal matters.

  a. universal

  b. dual

  c. designated

  d. special

36. Which of the following statements is true?

  a. A licensee may be held responsible for misrepresentations made by sellers if the licensee fails perform due diligence to verify the seller's information.

  b. In many states a property condition statement must be filled out by a seller of a residential property consisting of 1 to 5 dwelling units.

  c. In many states a property condition statement must be filled out by a seller of a residential property consisting of 1 to 10 dwelling units.

  d. The seller of a residential property built before 1988 must disclose any knowledge he or she has about whether lead-based paint was used in the dwelling unit and must provide the buyer with an EPA pamphlet titled *Protect Your Family From Lead In Your Home*.

37. A unilateral contract is

  a. a contract that has not yet been fully performed by one or both parties.

  b. a contract not expressed in words, but, through action or inaction, understood by the parties.

  c. a contract in which only one party gives a promise.

  d. a contract stated in words, written or oral.

38. Subrogation is

  a. the relegation of a party to a lesser right or security

  b. the substitution of one party for another in regard to pursuing a legal right, interest, or obligation

  c. a court order that requires a person to perform according to the terms of a contract

  d. the act of detaching an item of real property that changes the item to personal property, such as the cutting down of a natural tree

39. If, after _____, it is found that a trust fund account balance is greater than it should be, there is a _____.

  a. reconciliation, trust fund shortage

b. reconciliation, conversion

c. a commingling, conversion

d. reconciliation, trust fund overage

40. Gary has just arranged to obtain a home equity line of credit of 80% of the appraised value of his home, minus the total indebtedness against his home. The appraised value of his home is $200,000. The line of credit is $60,000. What is the total indebtedness against Gary's home?

a. $80,000

b. $100,000

c. $175,000

d. None of the above

41. Covenants, conditions, and restrictions (CC&Rs) are

a. city-wide plans that address such issues as transportation, housing, conservation, open spaces, noise, and safety on a county- or city-wide scale

b. detailed maps showing the boundaries of the individual parcels, streets, easements, engineering data, and, often, the environmental impact of the development

c. typically enforced by homeowners associations

d. reports containing pertinent information about the subdivision and that discloses to the prospective buyer that he or she has a minimum of 7 days in which to rescind the purchase agreement

42. If, at the end of a life estate, the future interest arises in any person other than the grantor, the residue of the estate is called a

a. remainder

b. reversion

c. subsequent condition

d. fee simple defeasible

43. Zoning regulations are instances of

a. eminent domain

b. escheat

c. police power

d. inverse condemnation

44. The value of a property at the end of its useful life refers to the property's

a. condemnation value

b. book value

c. salvage value

d. assessed value

45. Which of the following statements is true?

a. The Homeowner's Protection Act does not apply to FHA-insured loans.

b. The Homeowner's Protection Act requires that PMI on conventional loans be canceled when the mortgage balance reaches 80% of the property value and the borrower is current on the loan

c. PMI insurers the borrower.

d. PMI covers the top 50% of loans in case of default.

46. An agent who represents only one party in a given transaction is a

a. subagent

b. general agent

c. single agent

d. special agent

47. A stigmatized property is

a. a property in which one of the structures is in violation of the applicable zoning ordinances

b. a property with a termite problem

c. a property located in a floodplain

d. a property having a condition that certain persons may find materially negative in a way that does not relate to the property's actual physical condition

48. An agreement that is (or was) valid but is such that a court will not enforce it is

a. a valid contract

b. an unenforceable contract

c. a void contract

d. an oral contract

49. A bequest is a

a. transfer by will of personal property

b. transfer by will of real property

c. transfer by intestate succession of personal property

d. transfer by intestate succession of real property

50. The grant deed is most commonly used in which part of the country?

a. West

b. Midwest

c. South

d. East

51. What United States Supreme Court case held that the Civil Rights Act of 1866 prohibited all racial discrimination, whether private or public, in the sale or rental of either real or personal property?

a. *Shelley v. Kraemer*

b. *Jones v. Mayer*

c. *Jones v. Jones*

d. *Blankenship v. Myers*

52. The selling price of the home Howard is purchasing $280,000. The lender is willing to loan 80% of the lesser of the purchase price or the appraised value. If the amount the lender is willing to loan is $220,000, what is the appraised value of Howard's home?

a. $224,000

b. $275,000

c. $220,000

d. $160,000

53. Using straight-line depreciation, the depreciable life of a nonresidential income-producing property is how many years?

a. 39

b. 27½

c. 25

d. 25½

54. Amanda's house is located in Lot 6, Block E at Green Valley, Happy County. This legal description is based on which system?

a. recorded plat system

b. metes and bounds system

c. U.S. government survey system

d. rectangular system

55. Most locales have an administrative body referred to as _____, which entertains petitions for zoning exceptions and changes.

a. a planning commission

b. a Board of Supervisors

c. a zoning appeal board

d. an assessor's office

56. That the value of a property will tend toward the cost of comparable properties refers to the principle of

    a. conformity

    b. anticipation

    c. substitution

    d. integration

57. A loan under which periodic payments consist of interest only is

    a. a level payment loan

    b. a negative amortized loan

    c. a fully amortized loan

    d. an interest-only loan

58. A listing agent who is a dual agent

    a. owes fiduciary duties to the seller but not to the buyer

    b. owes fiduciary duties to the buyer but not to the seller

    c. owes fiduciary duties to both the buyer and to the seller

    d. owes only a duty to act fairly to both the buyer and to the seller

59. State laws differ as to whether a seller of a single-family home must disclose that

    a. the roof leaks when it rains

    b. a prior owner died of AIDS in the house

    c. the seller is a Christian

    d. the air conditioner doesn't work

60. Essential elements for the existence of a valid contract include

    a. a writing

    b. mutual consent

    c. impossibility of performance

    d. none of the above

61. Which of the following statements is false?

    a. A novation never relieves the assignor of liability under the original contract.

b. The policy behind the statute of limitations is that anyone who "slumbers upon his rights" may lose the right to bring an action.

c. An ironclad merger clause is a contract provision stating that no prior agreement or contemporaneous oral agreement will have any force or effect.

d. A contract can be discharged if the object or purpose of the contract becomes illegal.

62. Which of the following contains the fewest warranties?

a. a grant deed

b. a special warranty deed

c. a general warranty deed

d. a sheriff's deed

63. The Federal Fair Housing Act does not prohibit

a. discriminatory advertising, sales, or loan terms

b. a private club, which, incident to its primary purpose, provides lodging for other than a commercial purpose, from limiting the rental or occupancy of such lodging to members

c. retaliation against, or intimidation of, anyone making a fair-housing complaint

d. representing that prices will decline, or crime increase, or other negative effects will occur because of the entrance of minorities into particular areas

64. Stephen makes payments of $1,275 per month, including 4% interest on a fixed-rate, fully amortized 15-year loan. What was the initial amount of his loan?

Monthly Payment Per $1,000 on Fixed-Rate, Fully Amortized Loans				
Rate	10-year term	15-year term	30-year term	40-year term
4%	10.125	7.397	4.775	4.180
5%	10.607	7.908	5.369	4.822
6%	11.102	8.439	5.996	5.503
7%	11.611	8.989	6.653	6.215
8%	12.133	9.557	7.338	6.954

a. $305,024

b. $267,016

c. $172,367

d. none of the above

65. How many square feet are there in an acre?

a. 5,280

b. 43,560

c. 4,365

d. 43,650

66. Areas that are soaked or flooded by surface or groundwater frequently enough or for sufficient duration to support plants, birds, animals, and aquatic life are referred to as.

a. floodplains

b. coastal zones

c. wetlands

d. negative impact areas

67. Which appraisal approach is the best method for appraising single-family homes for which there is a ready market of similar properties?

a. replacement cost approach

b. summation approach

c. income approach

d. market data approach

68. A negative amortized loan is

a. a loan under which the mortgage payments pay all of the interest due but not enough of the principal to fully pay off the loan at the end of the loan term

b. a loan by which the installment payments do not cover all of the interest due — the unpaid part of the interest due being tacked onto the principal, thereby causing the principal to grow as each month goes by

c. a loan wherein the payments are sufficient to pay off the entire loan by the end of the loan term

d. a loan wherein periodic payments consist of interest only

69. A dual agent

a. owes a duty to act fairly to the buyer but not to the seller

b. owes a duty to act fairly both the buyer and to the seller

c. owes a duty to act fairly to the seller but not to the buyer

d. does not need to act fairly to either the seller or to the buyer

70. Until all contingencies in a real estate purchase agreement are met, the agreement is

a. void

b. enforceable

c. unenforceable

d. unilateral and executed

71. An escalator clause is

a. a clause providing for additional rent based on a percent of the tenant's gross receipts

b. a clause that provides for the tenant making certain improvements at the tenant's expense

c. a clause that states that the tenant must pay for 50% of the property taxes on the leased premises

d. a provision in a lease that provides for periodic increases in rent in an amount based on some objective criteria not in control of either the tenant or the landlord, such as the Consumer Price Index

72. Mortgage interest is usually paid in _____, in which case the seller would be _____for the portion of the month before closing.

a. advance, credited

b. advance, debited

c. arrears, credited

d. arrears, debited

73. Which of the following statements is true?

a. Because under antitrust law, a real estate office is usually considered to be an individual entity for antitrust purposes, a real estate office may assign salespersons to work specific areas.

b. It would be legal for a state to pass a law requiring brokers not to discount their commissions below 2% of sales price.

c. Under the Sherman Act, the term "group action" refers to three or more persons agreeing to act.

d. An MLS may refuse membership to a broker who discounts fees beyond a certain point.

74. Ernesto sold his house, receiving $423,000 after paying a 6% commission. For how much did Ernesto sell his house?

a. $400,000

b. $423,000

c. $475,000

d. none of the above

75. A landowner

a. may sell mineral rights separately from the rest of the property

b. may not sell mineral rights separately from the rest of the property

c. has no rights to minerals beneath his or her land

d. has rights to minerals that lay only within 100 feet of the surface of the property

76. The seller (or lessor) of a residential dwelling unit built before _____ must notify a buyer (or tenant) in writing about required disclosures for lead-based paint.

    a. 1968

    b. 1978

    c. 1988

    d. 1998

77. The straight-line method of depreciation calculates the amount of annual depreciation by dividing the cost of the improvement by

    a. the estimated physical life of the improvement

    b. 38 years

    c. the estimated useful life of the improvement

    d. 25½ years

78. In an adjustable-rate mortgage, the index is

    a. the benchmark rate of interest that is adjusted periodically

    b. a number of percentage points, usually fixed over the life of the loan

    c. an initial rate is called a discounted rate (also referred to as a teaser rate)

    d. equal to the margin minus the fully indexed rate

79. Agency by _____ may be created if someone reasonably believes that someone else is acting as his or her agent, and the supposed agent fails to correct the impression.

    a. implication

    b. ratification

    c. express agreement

    d. the equal dignities rule

80. A graduated lease is also referred to as a

    a. net lease

    b. triple net lease

    c. step-up lease

    d. gross lease

81. A lease often used in shopping centers that provides for the tenant's to pay a base rent amount plus a percentage of the gross receipts of the tenants' businesses is a

    a. graduated lease

b. percentage lease

c. triple net lease

d. net lease

82. The greater an individual's income, the higher the tax rate on that individual's income is an aspect of what kind of tax?

a. ad valorem

b. regressive

c. repressive

d. progressive

83. The Federal Fair Housing Act

a. prohibits directing people of protected classes away from, or toward, particular areas

b. prohibits religious organizations from limiting the sale, rental or occupancy of dwellings to persons of the same religion

c. prohibits a private club, which, incident to its primary purpose, provides lodging for other than a commercial purpose, from limiting the rental or occupancy of such lodging to members

d. limit the applicability of any reasonable local, State or Federal restrictions regarding the maximum number of occupants permitted to occupy a dwelling

84. The estimated cost to reproduce an office building with an estimated useful life of 40 years is $2,500,000. The land the building is on is valued at $850,000. Using the straight-line method of depreciation, what is the value of the property, assuming the actual age of the building is 12 years.

a. $1,750,000

b. $1,650,000

c. $2,437,500

d. none of the above

85. Judgment liens are _____ and _____ liens.

a. specific, involuntary

b. general, involuntary

c. specific, voluntary

d. general, voluntary

86. A city passed an ordinance to keep an industrial area separated from a residential area by an intervening commercial area. This is an example of a

a. variance

b. buffer zone

c. inclusionary zoning

d. spot zoning

87. Loss in value due to changes in zoning laws is referred to as

    a. functional obsolescence

    b. economic obsolescence

    c. physical obsolescence

    d. deferred obsolescence

88. Loss in value due to proximity to undesirable influences such as airport flight patterns is referred to as

    a. physical obsolescence

    b. functional obsolescence

    c. economic obsolescence

    d. deferred obsolescence

89. One of the advantages of an FHA-insured loan is

    a. relatively high LTVs

    b. relatively low loan amounts that can be insured

    c. upfront mortgage insurance premium (upfront MIP) and annual MIP premiums

    d. requires that properties meet certain minimum standards as determined by an FHA-approved appraiser

90. Which of the following statements is false?

    a. A designated agent is an agent who's principal intentionally, or by want of ordinary care, causes a third person to believe another to be his agent who is not actually employed by the principal.

    b. A subagent is an agent of an agent.

    c. A dual agent is a real estate broker who represents both the buyer and the seller in a real estate transaction.

    d. A single agent is an agent who represents only one person in a given transaction.

91. The federal law that specifically addresses property sites contaminated with hazardous waste is the

    a. Flood Control Act

    b. Interstate Land Sales full Disclosure Act

    c. Comprehensive Environmental Response, Compensation, and Liability Act

d. Truth-in-Lending Act

92. A lease with an obligation to purchase is a

    a. bilateral executed contract

    b. unilateral executed contract

    c. unilateral executory contract

    d. none of the above

93. Which of the following items related to a homeowner's personal residence are deductible from federal income tax?

    a. private mortgage insurance

    b. repairs on the residence

    c. property taxes paid on the residence

    d. maintenance and other operating expenses of owning a principal place of residence

94. The American with Disabilities Act (ADA) does not prohibit discrimination against persons with an impairment caused by

    a. blindness

    b. mental illness

    c. substance abuse

    d. loss of both legs, resulting from an accident while driving the getaway car during a bank robbery

95. The CAN-SPAM Act

    a. covers only bulk email messages

    b. exempts transactional emails

    c. covers commercial telephone calls as well as emails

    d. covers only emails sent intrastate

96. Which of the following statements is false?

    a. As in fraud, to find a violation of antitrust laws a plaintiff (in a civil action) or a prosecutor (in a criminal action) must establish that there was an intention to violate the law.

    b. The civil penalties for antitrust violations can be very high.

    c. The criminal penalties for antitrust violations can be very severe.

    d. It is easy to unintentionally violate antitrust laws.

97. The annual net operating income of Joel's apartment building is $210,000. An appraiser estimated the value of the property at $2,625,000. What capitalization rate did the appraiser use to arrive at her valuation?

a. 16%

b. 8%

c. 4 %

d. none of the above

98. Lien priority refers to

a. the dates on which the liens were recorded

b. the dates on which the liens were created

c. the order in which lien holders are paid if property is sold to satisfy a debt

d. the fact that state and federal liens have priority over judgment liens

99. Freehold estates other than _____ can always be inherited.

a. fee simple defeasible estates

b. leasehold estates

c. life estates

d. estates from period to period

100. Asbestos is associated with

a. radon

b. formaldehyde

c. mold

d. mesothelioma

101. Persons eligible for a VA-guaranteed loan must apply to the VA for a

a. Certificate of Honorable Discharge

b. Certificate of Adequate Value

c. Certificate of Eligibility

d. Certificate of Proper Service

102. If a purchase contract contains an assumption clause,

a. the borrower may sell off individual parcels and pay back only a proportionate amount of the loan

b. the original borrower remains primarily liable for the debt

c. the borrower may prepay the loan without incurring a prepayment penalty

d. the purchaser agrees to be primarily liable on the loan

103. Which of the following statements is false?

a. Usually, an agency relationship is created by express agreement between the principal and the agent.

b. By accepting or retaining the benefit of an act made by an unauthorized agent or by an agent who has exceeded his or her authority, a principal can create an agency by ratification.

c. An express agreement can only be created by a written contract.

d. Agency by implication may be created if someone reasonably believes that someone else is acting as his or her agent, and the supposed agent fails to correct the impression.

104. Statutory law is

a. law developed over time by tradition and law courts

b. law enacted by legislation

c. not one of the sets of laws that govern agency law

d. only enacted by state legislatures, not by the federal government

105. Which of the following statements is true?

a. An agent's client is also referred to as the agent's customer.

b. A salesperson is a dual agent of the supervising broker's client.

c. An agent for a particular transaction is a special agent

d. A dual agent is an agent given power of attorney to act on behalf of a principal for an unlimited range of legal matters.

106. A purchase contract contains a provision that states that the contract will not be binding if the sellers fail to obtain financing for the home into which they plan to move. This provision is called a

a. revocation clause

b. safety clause

c. contingency clause

d. rescission clause

107. Which of the following statements is false?

a. A contingency is an event that may, but is not certain to, happen, the occurrence upon which the happening of another event is dependent.

b. A net listing can take the form of any of the three basic types of listings: open, exclusive agency, or exclusive right to sell.

c. An open listing can be given to only one broker.

104

d. An offer must be accepted as stated — any change will be construed as a rejection of the entire offer.

108. The penalty for a first violation of the Federal Fair Housing Act can be up to
    a. $50,000
    b. $100,000
    c. $150,000
    d. $500,000

109. A method of avoiding foreclosure by conveying to a lender title to the property is a
    a. short sale
    b. non-strict foreclosure
    c. deed in lieu of foreclosure
    d. modified foreclosure

110. Ronald entered into a contract to sell his condo to Bob. Just prior to closing, Ronald breaches the agreement and refuses to complete the transaction. Bob decides that he doesn't want to force Ronald to go through with the deal — he just wants to tear up the contract and get all of his money back. What Bob wants is called
    a. specific performance
    b. arbitration
    c. rescission
    d. injunction

ANSWERS TO PRACTICE EXAM #2:

Note: If you would like to obtain a deeper understanding of the real estate principles behind the answers to the ***national*** portion of the exam, please consult the supplemental textbook *PSI Real Estate Exam Prep 2015-2016*, which provides a thorough, up-to-date review of the real estate principles covered in the ***national*** portion of the Pennsylvania real estate exam. This textbook is available both in print and Kindle formats on Amazon.com.

1.   **a.** Since 1958, Pennsylvania has required that a "coal severance notice" be conveyed in every deed, land sale agreement, and other documents if the rights to mine coal on the property have been transferred to another.

2.   **d.** Pennsylvania does not use the rectangular survey system, which is also referred to as the government survey system.

3.   **b.** Pennsylvania has adopted the two common law categories of fee simple defeasible estates: fee simple determinable and fee simple subject to a condition subsequent. A fee simple determinable is an estate that automatically reverts to the grantor upon the occurrence of a specified event with no need to take court action. A fee simple subject to a condition subsequent is an estate that, upon the noncompliance of the stated condition, the grantor or the grantor's successors in interest would have the right to terminate the preceding estate but must take court action to assert the right of termination and reversion. "So long as" are considered special limiting words used to convey a fee simple determinable.

4.   **b.** Pennsylvania's Probate, Estates, and Fiduciaries Code creates a legal life estate in a surviving spouse equal to one third of the value of the deceased spouse's estate, which one third interest the deceased spouse may not by will convey to another.

5.   **a.** Although Martha did not personally make prescriptive use of Emily's property for the 21 years required by Pennsylvania law, Pennsylvania recognizes "tacking," which allows a party to tack on to the prescriptive use of second party from whom the first party is a successor in interest.

6.   **b.** Although in general a month-to-month periodic tenancy requires a 15-day notice, if rent is not paid after a demand is made, only a 10-day notice is required. Pennsylvania Landlord and Tenant Act §250.501(b).

7.   **d.** The right to subjacent support is important in Pennsylvania because of Pennsylvania's vast coal, oil, and (recently) shale reserves. As an example, if a pipeline is placed on Pennsylvania land, it would be wise for the pipeline owners to negotiate for any subjacent support rights that may have been (and likely were) severed from the surface estate when the mineral rights to any land that the pipeline crosses over were acquired.

8.   **d.** Pursuant to the Pennsylvania Uniform Condominium Act, such a conversion notice must be given no later than one year before the tenant is required to vacate.

9.   **d.** Pennsylvania Rules of Civil Procedure §2950 et seq. provides that a confession of judgment is not valid if it is part of an instrument executed in connection with a transaction in which the party to whom credit is extended is a natural person and the money, property, or services that are the subject of the transaction are primarily for personal, family, or household purposes.

10.   **a.** Chapter 56 of the Pennsylvania Consolidated Statutes provides that a power of attorney is presumed to be durable and must be witnessed by *two* individuals, each of whom is 18 years of age or older

11.   **d.** Under Pennsylvania law, if the testator signs the will, the will need not be witnessed.

12.   **a.** Only choice a is false. Pennsylvania's Electronic Transactions Act requires for its application that the parties to a transaction must agree to conduct the transaction by electronic means.

13.   **b.** Although many states provide for some statutory period in which to redeem property after a foreclosure sale, Pennsylvania does not.

14.   **c.** Section 35.202 of Pennsylvania's Rules and Regulations of the State Real Estate Commission states as one of the exceptions to the requirement of a license is an owner of real estate with respect to property owned or leased by the owner. In the case of a corporation or partnership, this exclusion does not extend to more than five of the partnership's partners or the corporation's officers, nor to the other employees of the partnership or corporation.

15.   **b.** Section 455.608c of Pennsylvania's and Regulations of the State Real Estate Commission provides that a comparative market analysis must contain a disclosure statement that states, among other things, that the analysis has *not* been performed in accordance with the Uniform Standards of Professional Appraisal Practice.

16.   **d.** Section 35.288 of Pennsylvania's Rules and Regulations of the State Real Estate Commission provides that a licensee who sells his or her own real estate must inform the purchaser that the licensee is a real estate licensee.

17.   **d.** The statements in both a and b are false. Section 455.608c of Pennsylvania's Rules and Regulations of the State Real Estate Commission provides that a comparative market analysis must contain a disclosure statement that states, among other things, that the comparative market analysis has *not* been performed in accordance with the Uniform Standards of Professional Appraisal Practice. Additionally, section 35.281(b)(2) of Pennsylvania's Rules and Regulations of the State Real Estate Commission states: "*Open listing agreements* or nonexclusive buyer agency agreements *may be oral* if the seller/buyer or landlord/tenant is provided with a written memorandum stating the terms of the agreement."

18.   **c.** Section 35.32 (c) of Pennsylvania's Rules and Regulations of the State Real Estate Commission states that both choices a and b are correct.

19.   **c.** The Seller's Property Disclosure Statement contained in Section 35.335a of Pennsylvania's Rules and Regulations of the State Real Estate Commission states that the fact that a structural element, system or subsystem is near, at or beyond the end of its normal useful life is *not* by itself a material defect.

20.   **a.** Section 35.334 of Pennsylvania's Rules and Regulations of the State Real Estate Commission provides that before an agreement of sale is executed, the brokers involved in the transaction shall provide each party with a written estimate of reasonably foreseeable expenses associated with the sale that the party may be expected to pay.

21.   **d.** Section 455.604(12) of Pennsylvania's Real Estate Licensing and Registration Act (RELRA) states that accepting a commission or any valuable consideration by a salesperson or associate broker for the performance of any acts requiring a real estate license is prohibited except from the licensed real estate broker with whom the salesperson or associate broker is affiliated.

22.   **c.** Pennsylvania law provides for transaction licensee status, under which a licensee must be a licensed salesperson or broker but does *not* act as an agent of either party and does not owe a fiduciary duty to either party. *See*, §455.201 of Pennsylvania's Real Estate Licensing and Registration Act (RELRA).

23.   **a.** Although some states that permit designated agency do not see the broker as a dual agent if the broker remains totally uninvolved in the transaction, Section 35.315(e)(4) of Pennsylvania's Rules and Regulations of the State Real Estate Commission provides that the broker is a dual agent and must be disclosed as such to the parties to the transaction.

24.   **d.** Each of the persons in a-c must have a license or registration certificate. *See*, RELRA §455.303. Building-owner salespersons do not, however, have an education requirement.

25.   **b.** Pursuant to RELRA §455.532(b), qualifications for a cemetery broker's license include 60 hours of real estate instruction areas of study prescribed by the Commission.

26.   **b.** Pursuant to RELRA §455.606a(7), Joan must disclose to Mike any conflict of interest. The other choices presented are false, which can be confirmed by examining other subsections of §455.606.a.

27.   **c.** Pursuant to Pennsylvania Rules and Regulations of the Real Estate Commission §305(c), an advertisement by an associate broker, salesperson, cemetery associate broker or cemetery salesperson must contain the business name and telephone number of the employing broker. Additionally, the names and telephone numbers must be of equal size.

28.   **b.** Pursuant to RELRA §455.303, any person who is found guilty of carrying on business activities restricted to a Pennsylvania real estate licensee without having a valid license may, after conviction of the second offense, be sentenced to pay a fine not less than $2,000 but not more than $5,000 or to imprisonment for not less than one year but not more than two years, or both.

29.   **c.** Pursuant to RELRA §455.604(a)(6), a broker must preserve records relating to a real estate transaction for at least *three* years after consummation of the transaction. Pursuant to RELRA §455.404a(e)(1), licenses may be placed on inactive status for no more than *five* years.

30.   **a.** Pursuant to Pennsylvania Rules and Regulations of the State Real Estate Commission §35.281(b)1), open listing agreements or nonexclusive buyer agency agreements may be oral if the seller/buyer or landlord/tenant is provided with a written memorandum stating the terms of the agreement.

31.   **d.** The standard five tests for a fixture are method of attachment, adaptability of the attached item, relationship of the parties, intent of the person attaching the item, and agreement between the parties.

32.   **c.** Eminent domain is a right of the state to take, through due process proceedings (often referred to as condemnation proceedings), private property for public use upon payment of just compensation.

33.   **c.** Scarcity refers to a lack of abundance and is a key component of the theory that supply and demand drive market prices.

34.   **c.** A discount point is equal to 1% of the loan amount, not of the purchase price.

35.   **a.** A universal agent is an agent given power of attorney to act on behalf of a principal for an unlimited range of legal matters.

36.   **a.** A licensee may be held responsible for misrepresentations made by sellers if the licensee fails perform due diligence to verify the seller's information.

37.   **c.** A unilateral contract is a contract in which only one party gives a promise.

38.   **b.** Subrogation is the substitution of one party for another in regard to pursuing a legal right, interest, or obligation.

39.   **d.** If, after reconciliation, it is found that a trust fund account balance is greater than it should be, there is a trust fund overage.

40.   **b.** ($200,000 × .8) - (total indebtedness against the home) = $60,000.
$160,000 - (total indebtedness against the home) = $60,000.
Total indebtedness against the home = $100,000.

41.   **c.** CC&Rs are typically enforced by homeowners associations.

42.   **a.** If, at the end of a life estate, the future interest arises in any person other than the grantor, the residue of the estate is called a remainder.

43.   **c.** Examples of the use of police power in regard to real property include the creation and enforcement of zoning codes, building codes, subdivision regulations, and property setbacks.

44.   **c.** Salvage value (also referred to as residual value or scrap value) is the value of a property at the end of the property's useful life.

45.   **a.** HPA does not apply to FHA-insured or VA-guaranteed loans.

46.   **c.** A single agent is an agent who represents only one party in a given transaction.

47.   **d.** A stigmatized property is a property having a condition that certain persons may find materially negative in a way that does not relate to the property's actual physical condition.

48.   **b.** An unenforceable contract is (or was) valid but is such that a court will not enforce it. For example, pursuant to the statute of limitations, a contract that originally was valid and fully enforceable may become unenforceable after the passage of a certain amount of time.

49.   **a.** The transfer by will of personal property is known as a bequest.

50.   **a.** In a few states (primarily in the West, such as California), a grant deed is the most commonly used deed.

51.   **b.** In the 1968 landmark case of *Jones v. Mayer*, the United States Supreme Court held that the Civil Rights Act of 1866 prohibited all racial discrimination, whether private or public, in the sale or rental of either real or personal property.

52.   **b.** (the lesser of the appraised value or $280,000) × .8 = $220,000.
(the lesser of the appraised value or $280,000) = $220,000 ÷ .8 = $275,000.
Therefore, the appraised value of the home is $275,000.

53.   **a.** As a general rule, real property is depreciated in equal annual amounts (i.e., straight-line depreciation) over the depreciable life of the property, which for residential rental properties is 27½ years, and for nonresidential properties is 39 years.

54.   **a.** The recorded plat system is also referred to as the lot, block, and tract system because it describes locations using lot, block, and tract numbers.

55.   **c.** Most locales have an administrative body referred to as a zoning appeal board, which entertains petitions for zoning exceptions and changes.

56.   **c.** The principle of substitution states that the value of a property will tend toward the cost of a comparable, or of an equally desirable, substitute property.

57.   **d.** A loan under which periodic payments consist of interest only is a term loan (also referred to as a straight loan or an interest-only loan).

58.   **c.** A listing agent who is a dual agent owes fiduciary duties to both the buyer and the seller.

59.   **b.** Some states have exempted certain facts — such as long-ago deaths on the property or the property having been inhabited by a resident who committed suicide or who had AIDS or is HIV-positive — from required disclosures.

60.   **b.** Essential elements for the existence of a valid contract are (1) parties capable of contracting, (2) mutual consent, (3) lawful object or purpose, and (4) adequate consideration.

61.   **a.** A novation is the substitution of one party for another (in which case the first party is entirely excused from performing under the contract) or the substitution of one contract for another with the intent of extinguishing the original contract.

62.   **d.** A sheriff's deed contains no warranties and transfers only the former owner's interest, if any, in the property.

63.   **b.** The FFHA does not prohibit a private club, which, incident to its primary purpose, provides lodging for other than a commercial purpose, from limiting the rental or occupancy of such lodging to members.

64.   **c.** Finding where 4% and a 15-year term intersect in the table, we obtain the number $7.397 which is the dollar amount per month per $1,000 of the initial loan.
$7.397/$1,000 = $1,275/loan amount. Therefore,
loan amount = ($1,275 ÷ $7.397) × $1,000 = $172,367.

65.   **b.** An acre contains 43,560 square feet.

66.   **c.** The EPA defines wetlands as "areas that are soaked or flooded by surface or groundwater frequently enough or for sufficient duration to support plants, birds, animals, and aquatic life."

67.   **d.** The market or sales comparison approach (also known as the market data approach) is the best method for appraising land, residences, and other properties for which there is a ready market of similar properties.

68.   **b.** A negative amortized loan is a loan by which the installment payments do not cover all of the interest due — the unpaid part of the interest due being tacked onto the principal, thereby causing the principal to grow as each month goes by.

69.   **b.** A dual agent owes fiduciary duties to both the buyer and to the seller. These fiduciary duties are greater than, but include, the duty to act fairly to both the buyer and to the seller.

70.   **c.** Until all contingencies in a purchase agreement are met, the agreement is unenforceable.

71.   **d.** An escalator clause a provision in a lease that provides for periodic increases in rent in an amount based on some objective criteria not in control of either the tenant or the landlord, such as the Consumer Price Index.

72.   **d.** Mortgage interest is usually paid in arrears, in which case the seller would be debited for the portion of the month before closing.

73.   **a.** Because a real estate office is usually considered to be an individual entity for antitrust purposes, a real estate office may assign salespersons to work specific areas — a practice called "farming."

74.   **d.** We are told that the price the house sold for minus the commission paid was $423,000. Therefore,
Sales Price - Commission = $423,000
Sales Price - (6% of Sales Price) = $423,000
Sales price - (.06 × Sales Price) = $423,000
.94 × Sales Price = $423,000
Finally, dividing both sides of the equation by .94, we get Sales Price = $450,000.

75.   **a.** Landowners have certain rights in minerals that lie directly beneath the surface of their property and may sell their mineral rights separately from the rest of their property.

76.   **b.** The seller (or lessor) of a residential dwelling unit built before 1978 must notify a buyer (or tenant) in writing about required disclosures for lead-based paint.

77.   **c.** The straight-line method of depreciation calculates the amount of annual depreciation by dividing the cost of the improvement by the estimated useful life of the improvement.

78.   **a.** In an adjustable-rate mortgage, the index is the benchmark rate of interest that is adjusted periodically according to the going rate of T-bills, LIBOR, or the like.

79.   **a.** Agency by implication may be created if someone reasonably believes that someone else is acting as his or her agent, and the supposed agent fails to correct the impression.

80.   **c.** A step-up lease (also referred to as a graduated lease) is similar to a gross lease except that it provides (in a lease provision referred to as an escalator clause) for periodic increases in the rent, often based on the Consumer Price Index.

81.   **b.** Under a percentage lease, which is often used in shopping centers, the tenant typically pays a base rent amount plus a percentage of the gross receipts of the tenant's business.

82.   **d.** Income taxes are progressive, meaning that the greater an individual's income, the higher the tax rate on that individual's income.

83.   **a.** The Federal Fair Housing Act prohibits directing people of protected classes away from, or toward, particular areas.

84.   **d.** Annual depreciation = cost to reproduce ÷ useful life in years.
Annual depreciation = $2,500,000 ÷ 40 = $62,500.
Accrued depreciation = $62,500 × 12 = $750,000.
Property value = (reproduction cost - accrued depreciation) + land value.
Property value = ($2,500,000 - $750,000) + $850,000 = $2,600,000.

85.   **b.** Judgment liens are general and involuntary liens.

86.   **b.** A buffer zone is a strip of land to separate, or to ease the transition from, one use to another, such as a park separating a residential zone from a commercial zone, or a commercial or industrial zone separating residential zones from busy streets or highways.

87.   **b.** Loss in value due to changes in zoning laws is referred to as economic or external obsolescence.

88.   **c.** Loss in value due to proximity to undesirable influences such as airport flight patterns is referred to as economic obsolescence.

89. **a.** Allowing relatively high LTVs is one of the advantages of an FHA-insured loan.

90. **a.** A designated agent is an agent authorized by a real estate broker to represent a specific principal to the exclusion of all other agents in the brokerage.

91. **c.** The Comprehensive Environmental Response, Compensation, and Liability Act is intended to clean up sites contaminated with pollutants and toxic wastes.

92. **d.** A lease-purchase is executory and bilateral because a lease is executory and bilateral.

93. **c.** Property taxes paid on the residence are deductible.

94. **c.** Impairment due to substance abuse is not covered by the ADA.

95. **b.** An email sent to a client or customer concerning an existing transaction or that updates the client or customer about an ongoing transaction is referred to in the law as a transactional email and is exempt from the CAN-SPAM rules.

96. **a.** Having a firm grasp of the basics of how antitrust laws impact a real estate agent's behavior is very important because it is easy to unintentionally violate antitrust laws and the penalties, both criminal and civil, can be very severe.

97. **b.** $210,000 ÷ $2,625,000 = 8%.

98. **c.** Lien priority refers to the order in which lien holders are paid if property is sold to satisfy a debt.

99. **c.** Freehold estates other than life estates are sometimes referred to as estates of inheritance because they always can be inherited.

100. **d.** As asbestos ages, it breaks down to small fibers that, if inhaled in sufficient quantity over sufficient time, can cause a variety of ailments, including a type of cancer known as mesothelioma.

101. **c.** Eligible persons must apply to the VA for a Certificate of Eligibility (can be done online), which the applicant must present to the lender.

102. **d.** In an assumption, the purchaser agrees to be primarily liable on the loan, but the original borrower remains secondarily liable in case the purchaser defaults, unless there is a complete novation, in which case the seller would be relieved of all responsibility.

103. **c.** Unless the statute of frauds requires that the agreement be in writing, an express agency agreement can be oral.

104. **b.** Statutory law is law enacted by legislation.

105. **c.** An agent for a particular act or transaction is a special agent.

106. **c.** A contingency clause is a contract provision that makes performance of a certain act conditional on the occurrence of a specified event.

107. **c.** An open listing agreement may be made by a seller to any number of brokers, though only one commission would be paid, going to the agent who first procurers an offer acceptable to the seller.

108. **a.** The penalty for a first violation of the FFHA can be up to $50,000; the penalty for each subsequent violation can be up to $100,000. These fines can be supplemented by other civil damages, injunctions, and reasonable attorney's fees and costs.

109. **c.** Surrendering a deed in lieu of foreclosure is a method of avoiding foreclosure by conveying to a lender title to a property in lieu of the lender's foreclosing on the property.

110.   **c.** Rescission extinguishes a contract and returns each party to the position it was in immediately prior to the formation of the contract.

PRACTICE EXAM #3:

Note: Questions 1-30 of this exam consist of *state-portion* questions of the Pennsylvania real estate exam. Questions 31-110 of this exam consist of *national-portion* questions of the Pennsylvania relics eight exam.

1. Downward displacement of surface materials caused by the collapse of coal mine shafts is referred to as

    a. lateral support dysfunction

    b. displacement of profit á prendre

    c. mine subsidence

    d. appurtenance displacement

2. Pennsylvania uses which of the following methods of legal land description?

    a. metes and bounds

    b. government survey system

    c. neither a nor b

    d. Both a and b

3. In Pennsylvania, fee simple defeasible estates can be

    a. fee simple defeasible subject to attachment

    b. fee simple determinable

    c. fee simple subject to a condition subsequent

    d. both b and c

4. Andrew's father conveys his condo to Andrew "during" the years 2015-2020. Andrew receives

    a. fee simple absolute

    b. fee simple determinable

    c. fee simple subject to a condition subsequent

    d. life estate

5. Joe, who lives in Pennsylvania, has been walking across Ben's backyard without Ben's approval every day for the past 15 years.

    a. Joe has a prescriptive easement.

    b. Joe does not have a prescriptive easement.

    c. Joe has a license to use.

    d. Joe has acquired a part of the backyard by attachment.

6. If a real estate licensee acting as an exclusive leasing agent is involved in a lease transaction for how many years may the term of the lease be if it is not in writing?

a. 3 years

b. 2 years

c .1 year

d. such a lease must be in writing.

7. In Pennsylvania, during the second and subsequent years of a residential lease, the maximum amount a landlord may require as a security deposit is

a. one-month's rent

b. two-month's rent

c. three-month's rent

d. six-month's rent

8. Under Pennsylvania law, which of the following is (are) false?

a. General partnerships can hold title to real property in the partnership name.

b. Limited partnerships can hold title to real property in the partnership name.

c. Neither a nor b.

d. Both a and b.

9. Bob hires a general contractor to build a single-family house on a Pennsylvania lot that Bob owns. Bob intends to live in the house when it is completed. Suppose further that Bob pays the general contractor the full contract price.

a. If the general contractor fails to pay a subcontractor the $550 owed to the subcontractor, the subcontractor has the right to file a mechanics lien.

b. If the general contractor fails to pay a subcontractor the $750 owed to the subcontractor, the subcontractor has the right to file a mechanics lien.

c. The subcontractor does not have the right to a mechanics lien.

d. Both a and b are true.

10. In Pennsylvania, an attorney-in-fact

a. may be a real estate salesperson

b. must be a licensed attorney

c. may, if so authorized by the principal, make medical decisions on behalf of the principal

d. both a and c

11. Which, if any, of the following wills are not recognized in Pennsylvania if the testator was domiciled in Pennsylvania at the time of the execution of the will?

a. holographic wills

b. nuncupative wills

c. neither a nor b

d. both a and b

12. Real estate licensees in Pennsylvania may

a. fill in the blanks in a preprinted real estate sales agreement

b. give legal advice to their principals

c. write language to modify a real estate sales agreement

d. both a and c

13. Homeowners who qualify for loan assistance pursuant to Pennsylvania's Homeowner's Emergency Assistance Program (HEMAP) are required to pay up to what percent of their net monthly income toward their total housing expense?

a. 5-10%

b. 15-20%

c. 25-30%

d. 35-40%

14. Pennsylvania's Rules and Regulations of the State Real Estate Commission states that the individual broker responsible for the real estate transactions of a partnership, association, or corporation that holds a broker's license is

a. an associate broker

b. a transaction licensee

c. a broker of record

d. a manager of record

15. If a payment is made from the Real Estate Recovery Fund to settle a claim for an act of a licensee

a. the license of that licensee will be automatically suspended upon the date of the payment from the Real Estate Recovery Fund

b. the licensee will not be granted reinstatement until the licensee has repaid in full the exact amount paid from the Real Estate Recovery Fund

c. both a and b

d. neither a nor b

16. Escrow accounts established by brokers for holding funds received by parties to a real estate transaction

   a. must be maintained in a Federally-or State-insured bank or recognized depository

   b. must not provide for the withdrawal of funds without prior notice

   c. both a and b

   d. neither a nor b

17. Under Pennsylvania law, which, if any, of the following statements is false?

   a. Agency by implication may be created if someone reasonably believes that someone else is acting as his or her agent, and the supposed agent fails to correct the impression.

   b. In all real estate agency situations, a salesperson employed by a broker owes the same duties to the broker's principal as does the broker.

   c. Both a and b are false.

   d. Neither a nor b is false.

18. In Pennsylvania, an exclusive listing

   a. may not contain an automatic renewal clause

   b. may not contain a listing period greater than six months

   c. may contain authority of the broker to execute a signed agreement of sale or lease for the owner or lessor

   d. may contain an option by the broker to purchase the listed property

19. Under Pennsylvania law

   a. a material defect is a problem with the property or any portion of it that would have a significant adverse impact on the value of the residential real property or that involves an unreasonable risk to people on the land

   b. the fact that a structural element, system or subsystem is near, at or beyond the end of its normal useful life is by itself a material defect

   c. both a and b are true

   d. neither a nor b is true

20. The document that must be presented to a potential seller or buyer at the initial interview is

   a. Escrow instructions

   b. Consumer Notice

   c. Seller's Property Disclosure Statement

   d. Comparative market analysis

21. Ted is an associate broker employed by broker Kathy. Ted has worked with Kathy and with Kathy's cooperating broker, Julie, to make a sale of an apartment building. Ted may accept a commission for his work in this transaction

a. from Kathy

b. from Julie

c. from either Kathy or Julie

d. from either Kathy nor Julie

22. John is a transaction licensee who is working with a buyer and seller regarding the purchase of a home. Which, if any, of the following statements is (are) true?

a. John is an agent of the buyer.

b. John is an agent of the seller.

c. John must have a currently valid salesperson or broker license.

d. All of the statements a-c are true

23. Marvin is a broker who employs both Kathy and Mary as salespersons. Marvin designates Kathy as a designated agent for the seller and Mary as a designated agent for the buyer in regard to the sale of a home. Under Pennsylvania law,

a. Kathy owes fiduciary duties to the buyer.

b. Mary owes fiduciary duties to the seller.

c. Marvin owes fiduciary duties to both the seller and to the buyer.

d. None of the statements a-c are true.

24. In Pennsylvania, which, if any, of the following does (do) not need to satisfy an education requirement?

a. Rental listing referral agent.

b. Building-owner salesperson.

c. Campground membership salesperson.

d. Both a and b do not need to satisfy education requirement.

25. In Pennsylvania an individual who applies for a broker-owner salesperson license need not

a. satisfy any education requirement

b. be at least 21 years of age

c. have a good reputation for honesty and integrity

d. both a and b

26. No violation of the Real Estate Licensing and Registration Act (RELRA) on the part of any salesperson, associate broker, or other employee of any licensed broker shall be grounds

for the revocation or suspension of the license of the employing broker unless it appears at the Commission hearings held that

    a. such employing broker had constructive knowledge of such violation

    b. such employing broker had actual knowledge of such violation

    c. such employing broker acted promptly to discipline the violator

    d. such employing broker had properly supervised the violator

27. A salesperson's license

    a. may be kept by the salesperson at the salesperson's home and need not be displayed

    b. may be kept by the salesperson at home but must be displayed so that if a representative of the Commission visits, the license may readily be examined

    c. must be displayed in the employing broker's office in which the salesperson works

    d. must be displayed in the employing broker's main office

28. Any person who is found guilty of carrying on business activities restricted to a Pennsylvania real estate licensee without having a valid license may, after conviction of the first offense,

    a be sentenced to pay a fine not exceeding $500 and/or to be imprisoned for not more than 3 months

    b be sentenced to pay a fine not exceeding $1,000 and/or to be imprisoned for not more than 6 months

    c be sentenced to pay a fine not exceeding $2,000 and/or to be imprisoned for not more than 1 year

    d be sentenced to pay a fine not exceeding $5,000 and/or to be imprisoned for not more than 2 years

29. Pennsylvania real estate licenses may be placed on inactive status for no more than how many years?

    a. 7 years

    b. 5 years

    c. 3 years

    d. 2 years

30. Emily has had much experience investing in real estate, but is not a Pennsylvania real estate licensee. Emily's next-door neighbor, John, asks Emily to negotiate the sale of his house, and promises to pay Emily 3% of the sales price if she is successful. Emily successfully negotiates the sale for John, but John refuses to pay her anything.

    a. Emily could have been able to sue John for the agreed amount if the agreement had been in writing.

    b. Emily can file a mechanics lien in the amount of 3% of the sales price.

c. Emily cannot sue John for any services she rendered related to this transaction.

d. Emily cannot sue for the 3%, but she can sue for reasonable compensation for her time spent on the transaction.

31. The three broad categories of real property are

a. land, emblements, easements

b. land, improvements, things affixed to the land

c. land, situs, heterogeneity

d. land, appurtenances, things affixed to the land

32. Property taxes are

a. the main source of revenue for most local governments

b. based on the property owner's income

c. are a significant, but not primary, source of revenue for the federal government

d. are seldom used to fund schools

33. A property's ability to satisfy a potential buyer's need or desire refers to the property's

a. scarcity

b. utility

c. demand

d. transferability

34. Which of the following statements is false?

a. A high LTV can result in a loan being denied.

b. A high LTV can result in the lender's increasing the cost of the loan to the borrower.

c. A high LTV can result in the lender's requiring that the borrower pay for private mortgage insurance.

d. A high LTV is perceived as a low risk by lenders.

35. A _____ is an agent for a particular act or transaction.

a. specific agent

b. subagent

c. special agent

d. single agent

36. In many states, the seller of what kind of property is responsible for filling out a property disclosure statement?

a. all residential buildings

b. all residential and commercial buildings

c. residential properties consisting of 1 to 4 dwelling units and commercial buildings in which at least four people work

d. residential properties consisting of 1 to 4 dwelling units

37. In regard to extent of performance, a contract may be

a. bilateral or unilateral

b. executory or executed

c. express or implied

d. executed or implied

38. An examination of all relevant public documents to determine whether there exist any potential defects against the title is called

a. a quiet title action

b. a title plant

c. a title search

d. an opinion of title

39. Examples of trust funds do not include

a. security deposits made by a client's tenants

b. a broker's real estate commissions

c. funding for a client's loan

d. interest, if any, paid in a trust fund account

40. Evan purchased a rectangular lot measuring 125' deep by 160' along the street. Zoning regulations require a 15' setback from the street and a 10' setback along all other sides. What are the buildable dimensions of Evan's lot?

a. 115' × 145'

b. 110' × 140'

c. 100' × 140'

d. 115' × 145'

41. The Interstate Land Sales Full Disclosure Act requires that a developer provide each prospective buyer with a _____ that contains pertinent information about the subdivision and that discloses to the prospective buyer that he or she has a minimum of 7 days in which to rescind the purchase agreement.

a. master Plan

b. covenant

c. property Report

d. plat

42. Things affixed to the land are considered

a. personal property

b. emblements

c. real property

d. trade fixtures

43. Which of the following is not an example of police power?

a. Zoning codes

b. Eminent domain

c. Building codes

d. Subdivision regulations

44. The value placed on a property that is usually intended to estimate the market value of the property is referred to as the property's

a. assessed value

b. appraised value

c. salvage value

d. book value

45. Which of the following statements is false?

a. Private mortgage insurance (PMI) is insurance that lenders often require for loans with an LTV more than 80%.

b. PMI insurers the lender.

c. The Homeowner's Protection Act requires that PMI be canceled when the mortgage balance reaches 80% of the property value and the borrower is current on the loan.

d. PMI covers the top amount of a loan in case of default.

46. A _____ does not owe fiduciary duties to either party and is therefore not held to the same legal standards of conduct as is an agent.

a. dual agent

b. transactional broker

c. universal agent

d. ostensible agent

47. Many states require an agent to perform _____ to investigate a residential property consisting of 1 to 4 dwelling units to ensure that the property is as represented by the seller and to disclose accurate and complete information regarding the property to potential purchasers

    a. reconciliation

    b. due diligence

    c. ratification

    d. lis pendens

48. Consent to an agreement obtained by fraud may be

    a. rescinded by the party defrauded

    b. enforceable by the party who committed the fraud

    c. valid

    d. adequate

49. A contract provision that makes performance of a certain act conditional on the occurrence of a specified event is called a

    a. liquidated damages clause

    b. contingency clause

    c. severability clause

    d. safety clause

50. What Supreme Court case held that private racially-based restrictive covenants are invalid under the Fourteenth Amendment?

    a. *Jones v. Mayer*

    b. *Stuart v. Clarke*

    c. *Shelley v. Kraemer*

    d. *Maxwell v. Moormon*

51. Margaret is purchasing a home with a purchase price of $280,000 and an appraised value of $275,000. If the lender is willing to loan 80% of the lesser of the purchase price and the appraised value, how much will be Margaret's down payment?

    a. $60,000

    b. $56,000

    c. $55,000

    d. none of the above

52. The preference for a certain location is referred to as

    a. situs

b. fixity

c. heterogeneity

d. homogeneity

53. After a master plan is adopted, the local government implements the plan by use of all except which of the following?

   a. inverse condemnation

   b. eminent domain

   c. taxation

   d. police power

54. Real property, the expansion, redevelopment, or reuse of which may be complicated by the presence or potential presence of a hazardous substance, pollutant, or contaminant is referred to as

   a. natural hazard zones

   b. redevelopment sites

   c. brownfields

   d. blighted zones

55. The process of gathering together two or more parcels to make the whole more valuable than the sum of its parts is called

   a. change

   b. assemblage

   c. contribution

   d. anticipation

56. Which appraisal process obtains the market value of the subject property by adding the value of the land (unimproved) of the subject property to the depreciated value of the cost (if purchased at current prices) of the improvements on the subject property?

   a. market data approach

   b. replacement cost approach

   c. income approach

   d. sales comparison approach

57. Under an adjustable-rate mortgage, the benchmark rate of interest that is adjusted periodically is referred to as the

   a. discounted rate

   b. index

   c. margin

d. adjustment period

58. Under a reverse mortgage insured by the FHA, which of the following statements is false?

 a. The term "permanently leaves home" refers to 365 days of continuous absence.

 b. The homeowner is responsible for paying homeowners insurance premiums.

 c. The homeowner is responsible for maintaining the home in good repair.

 d. The homeowner is not responsible for paying property taxes.

59. An agency relationship created by a verbal agreement

 a. is against the statute of frauds

 b. is created by express agreement

 c. is created by ratification

 d. is created by implication

60. Which of the following statements is false?

 a. A subagent is an agent of an agent

 b. Ostensible agency is created when a principal intentionally, or by want of ordinary care, causes a third person to believe another to be his agent who is not actually employed by the principal.

 c. A dual agent is a real estate broker who represents both the seller and the buyer in a real estate transaction.

 d. A universal agent is an agent authorized by a real estate broker to represent a specific principal to the exclusion of all other agents in the brokerage.

61. If I offer to pay you $20 to mow my lawn on Tuesday and you agree to do so, our _____ contract remains _____ until both of us perform as agreed, at which time our contract becomes an _____ contract.

 a. unilateral, executory, executed

 b. bilateral, executed, executory

 c. bilateral, executory, executed

 d. unilateral, executed, executory

62. A listing agreement providing a broker with all proceeds received from the sale over a specified amount is

 a. an exclusive right to sell listing

 b. a net listing

 c. an open listing

 d. an exclusive agency listing

63. A lease constitutes in part an executory contract between the landlord and the tenant. This contract aspect of a lease creates between a landlord and the tenant

   a. privity of estate

   b. privity of contract

   c. privity of chattel

   d. privity of reversion

64. The statute of frauds requires that

   a. all contracts have sufficient consideration

   b. actions based on contracts must be brought within a certain time after the occurrence of a breach

   c. contracts of certain types must be in writing to be enforceable

   d. actions for specific performance cannot succeed for personal services

65. Which of the following statements is false?

   a. Under a gross lease the tenant leases land and agrees to construct a building or to make other significant improvement on the land.

   b. A graduated lease is similar to a gross lease except that it provides for periodic increases in the rent, often based on the Consumer Price Index.

   c. Under a percentage lease, which is often used in shopping centers, the tenant typically pays a base rent amount plus a percentage of the gross receipts of the tenant's business.

   d. Under a net lease, the tenant pays a fixed rental amount plus some of the landlord's operating expenses (such as a percent of property taxes).

66. Many states have a _____, under which a choice of either a judicial or nonjudicial foreclosure must be made

   a. judicial foreclosure rule

   b. nonjudicial foreclosure rule

   c. one-action rule

   d. limited choice rule

67. The Federal Fair Housing Act does not

   a. limit the applicability of any reasonable local, State or Federal restrictions regarding the maximum number of occupants permitted to occupy a dwelling

   b. prohibit refusal to loan in particular areas

   c. prohibit representing that prices will decline, or crime increase, or other negative effects will occur because of the entrance of minorities into particular areas

   d. prohibit discriminatory access to multiple listing services

68. Kathy is the supervising broker at the local branch of a large national brokerage. On June 1, she calls a meeting of all of her salespersons and associate brokers and instructs them that through the end of the year they were going to set their commissions at 5%, no more, no less. Her sales force subsequently complies. This is an example of

a. price-fixing

b. market allocation

c. group boycott

d. actions that do not violate the Sherman Act.

69. Stephen purchased a home for $200,000 with a 4 % fixed-rate, fully amortized 15-year loan in the principal amount of $172,367. He makes payments of $1,275 per month. What is the amount of unpaid principal on this loan after the first month's payment?

a. $171,258.67

b. $171,092.00

c. $171,666.56

d. none of the above

70. Tax advantages that homeowners do not enjoy include deductions for

a. real estate taxes

b. loan discount points that represent interest

c. FHA mortgage insurance premiums

d. mortgage interest

71. A non-possessory right to use a portion of another property owner's land for a specific purpose is

a. a support right

b. an emblement

c. an easement

d. an encroachment

72. What is associated with mesothelioma?

a. radon

b. mold

c. asbestos

d. formaldehyde

73. A church is permitted to relocate to an area zoned exclusively for residential properties. This is an example of

a. conditional use

b. variance

c. spot zoning

d. nonconforming use

74. Which appraisal approach is the best method for appraising land for which there is a ready market of similar properties?

a. replacement cost approach

b. summation approach

c. income approach

d. market data approach

75. One of the disadvantages of an FHA-insured loan is

a. the loans cannot have a prepayment penalty

b. lower FICO scores are required than are typically required by conventional loans

c. the loans are assumable upon approval by the FHA

d. that properties must meet certain minimum standards as determined by an FHA-approved appraiser

76. A buyer's agent who is a dual agent

a. owes fiduciary duties to the seller but not to the buyer

b. owes fiduciary duties to the buyer but not to the seller

c. owes fiduciary duties to both the buyer and to the seller

d. owes only a duty to act fairly to both the buyer and to the seller

77. Which of the following statements is false?

a. Some states permit a broker to act *not* as an agent who represents one or more parties to a real estate transaction, but to act as a mere middleman who brings the parties together and lets the parties do all of the negotiating among themselves.

b. An agent occupies a special legal relationship referred to as a fiduciary relationship to his or her principal.

c. There is a rule of equity known as estoppel that holds that one who causes another to rely on his or her words or actions shall be estopped (prohibited) from later taking a contrary position detrimental to the person who so relied.

d. A broker's principal is also referred to as the broker's customer.

78. The person who hires a broker to list and sell the person's real property is not referred to as the broker's

a. seller

b. client

c. principal

d. customer

79. An informal name for various federal and state laws that provide for the registration of sex offenders is

a. Stigmatized Property Disclosure Law

b. Sex Registration Law

c. Megan's Law

d. Mitchell's Law

80. Which of the following statements regarding the Residential Lead-Based Paint Hazard Reduction Act is false?

a. A seller (or lessor) of a residential dwelling unit built before 1978 must notify a buyer (or tenant) in writing about required disclosures for lead-based paint.

b. A lead-based paint hazard pamphlet must be given to prospective purchasers but not to tenants.

c. A seller must disclose knowledge that the seller has about whether lead-based paint was used in the dwelling.

d. A seller must offer a prospective buyer 10 days to inspect for lead-based paint and lead-based paint hazards.

81. If a tenant pays a fixed rental amount plus some of the landlord's operating expenses, the tenant has what kind of lease?

a. gross lease

b. net lease

c. graduated lease

d. ground lease

82. An agreement that provides for the purchase of property preceded by a lease under which a portion of each lease payment is applied to the purchase price is a

a. graduated-purchase agreement

b. net-purchase agreement

c. lease-purchase agreement

d. lease-option agreement

83. A legal doctrine that states that a legally enforceable relationship exists between persons who are parties to a valid agreement is

a. a leasehold interest that lies between a primary lease and a sublease

b. often referred to as profit á prendre

c. privity of contract

d. privity of estate

84. The escrow agent in charge of the closing of a real estate transaction must report the gross sale price and the seller's name and Social Security number to

a. FFHA

b. CERCLA

c. IRS

d. HUD

85. The Federal Fair Housing Act

a. prohibits discrimination against children with respect to properties occupied solely by persons 62 years of age or older

b. limits the applicability of any reasonable local, State or Federal restrictions regarding the maximum number of occupants permitted to occupy a dwelling

c. prohibits discrimination against children with respect to properties where at least 80% of the dwelling units are occupied by at least one person who is 55 years of age or older

d. prohibits discriminatory access to multiple listing services

86. Placing a number on the Do-Not-Call Registry prohibits

a. live calls from persons or entities with whom the customer has an established business relationship

b. Commercial calls from persons with whom the receivers of the calls have no established business relationship

c. calls for which the customer has given prior written permission

d. calls by or on behalf of tax-exempt, non-profit organizations

87. What would be the estimated market value of a subject lot measuring 110' × 140' if the following 3 comparables are used for the analysis?
Comparable 1: Measures 100' × 110', sold for $99,000.
Comparable 2: Measures 120' × 130', sold for $132,600.
Comparable 3: Measures 110' × 130', sold for $135,850

a. $138,000

b. $140,000

c. $150,000

d. none of the above

88. A lien is created to fund the installation of sidewalks and street lights on Elm Street, between Third and Vine. What type of lien is this?

a. mechanics lien

b. general lien

c. ad valorem real estate tax lien

d. special assessment lien

89. The primary characteristic that distinguishes a freehold estate from a non-freehold estate is

a. duration

b. cost

c. that only one type is measured by the life of a person

d. conditions subsequent

90. John sold Joe a vacant lot next to John's residence. The deed stated that the owner of the lot Joe was acquiring must maintain a party wall. This is an example of

a. an affirmative condition

b. an affirmative covenant

c. a negative condition

d. a negative covenant

91. Loss in value due to wear and tear of use is referred to as

a. functional obsolescence

b. physical obsolescence

c. external obsolescence

d. internal obsolescence

92. The capitalization rate for a property is calculated by

a. dividing the annual net income by the purchaser's actual cash investment in the property

b. dividing the annual net income by the purchase price of the property

c. dividing the purchase price of the property by the annual net income

d. dividing the annual gross income by the purchase price of the property

93. If a broker supplies financing to remodel a condo with the stipulation that the broker will have the listing to sell the condo,

a. the broker's agency is coupled with an interest

b. the seller may terminate the listing because agency is a personal relationship based on trust and confidence

c. the seller may terminate the agency because of the conflict of interest

d. the broker is what is referred to as a designated agent

94. The transfer by will of personal property is known as a

    a. devise

    b. legatee

    c. bequest

    d. nuncupative

95. What type of deed is used to convey title when no tangible consideration is given?

    a. sheriff's deed

    b. general warranty deed

    c. gift deed

    d. grant deed

96. Which of the following statements is false?

    a. An MLS organization may not set fees or commission splits for its members.

    b. Under the Sherman Act, "group action" refers to two or more persons agreeing to act.

    c. Under the Sherman Act, it is permissible for a broker to condition the sale of a property upon the broker's obtaining the listing for future sales.

    d. An antitrust conspiracy occurs when two or more persons agree to act and the agreed-upon action has the effect of restraining trade.

97. "Puffing" refers to

    a. a false promise

    b. concealment

    c. somewhat overblown sales talk

    d. intentional misrepresentation

98. An apartment building produces an annual gross income of $2,970,000. Vacancies and uncollectible rents are running 8%. Monthly operating expenses are $145,400. What is the annual NOI?

    a. $2,587,000

    b. $1,225,200

    c. $1,982,400

    d. none of the above

99. A property's bundle of rights does not include

    a. right of possession

b. right to use and enjoy

c. right of disposition

d. right to avoid special assessments

100. A loan under which periodic payments consist of interest only is a

a. straight loan

b. level payment loan

c. negative amortized loan

d. fully amortized loan

101. For a VA-guaranteed loan, the appraised value of the subject property is presented in a

a. Certificate of Eligibility

b. Certificate of Appraisal

c. Certificate of Property Value

d. Certificate of Reasonable Value

102. Which of the following statements is true?

a. In dual agency, conflicts of loyalty and confidentiality cannot arise.

b. Conversion is the act of placing funds belonging to clients or customers into accounts also holding the agent's funds.

c. If the seller wants to know whether the buyer is willing to pay a higher price, the listing agent who is a dual agent must not disclose a price concession from the buyer without the buyer's consent.

d. Conversion is the act of placing funds belonging to clients or customers into accounts also holding the agent's funds.

103. A court proceeding intended to establish the true ownership of a property, thereby eliminating any cloud on title is a

a. quiet title action

b. lis pendens

c. writ of attachment

d. foreclosure action

104. To be valid a deed need not

a. be in writing

b. be signed by the grantor

c. adequately describe the property

d. none of the above

105. Which of the following are not among the good-faith estimate (GFE) tolerance levels required to be included in the HUD-1 settlement form?

    a. charges that cannot increase

    b. charges that can increase

    c. charges that in the aggregate cannot increase more than 5%

    d. charges that in the aggregate cannot increase more than 10%

106. A common law legal concept developed by the courts to determine the proportioning of commissions among agents involved in a real estate transaction is referred to as

    a. proportional commissioning

    b. procuring cause

    c. commission partitioning

    d. diligence analysis

107. Three similar properties in the area have fair market values and monthly rentals as follows: Comparable 1 — $264,600; $980. Comparable 2 — $272,640; $960. Comparable 3; $283,200; $960. What is the average monthly gross rent multiplier for these properties?

    a. 283

    b. 284

    c. 295

    d. none of the above

108. Examples of general liens include

    a. mechanics liens, property tax liens, judgment liens

    b. property tax liens, special assessment liens, mortgage liens

    c. mechanics liens, property tax liens, federal income tax liens

    d. judgment liens, federal income tax liens, state income tax liens

109. Loans under which interest rates vary over the term of the loan are

    a. fully amortized loans

    b. negative amortized loans

    c. adjustable-rate loans

    d. partially amortized loans

110. Emily entered into a written contract to sell her condo to John, but John breached the contract and refused to go through with the sale. If Emily wants a court to order John to complete the sale, she should

a. seek rescission of the contract

b. seek liquidated damages

c. seek specific performance

d. seek compensatory damages

ANSWERS TO PRACTICE EXAM #3:

Note: If you would like to obtain a deeper understanding of the real estate principles behind the answers to the *national* portion of the exam, please consult the supplemental textbook *PSI Real Estate Exam Prep 2015-2016*, which provides a thorough, up-to-date review of the real estate principles covered in the *national* portion of the Pennsylvania real estate exam. This textbook is available both in print and Kindle formats on Amazon.com.

1.   **c.** Mine subsidence is the downward displacement of surface materials caused by the collapse of coal mine shafts. In 1961, Pennsylvania established the Mine Subsidence Insurance Fund to provide insurance against losses caused by mine subsidence.

2.   **a.** Pennsylvania does not use the government survey system as a legal land description.

3.   **d.** Pennsylvania has adopted the two common law categories of fee simple defeasible estates: fee simple determinable and fee simple subject to a condition subsequent. A fee simple determinable is an estate that automatically reverts to the grantor upon the occurrence of a specified event with no need to take court action. A fee simple subject to a condition subsequent is an estate that, upon the noncompliance of the stated condition, the grantor or the grantor's successors in interest would have the right to terminate the preceding estate but must take court action to assert the right of termination and reversion.

4.   **b.** Pennsylvania has adopted the two common law categories of fee simple defeasible estates: fee simple determinable and fee simple subject to a condition subsequent. A fee simple determinable is an estate that automatically reverts to the grantor upon the occurrence of a specified event with no need to take court action. A fee simple subject to a condition subsequent is an estate that, upon the noncompliance of the stated condition, the grantor or the grantor's successors in interest would have the right to terminate the preceding estate but must take court action to assert the right of termination and reversion. "During" is considered a special limiting word used to convey a fee simple determinable.

5.   **b.** In Pennsylvania, prescriptive use must be for 21 years.

6.   **d.** Real Estate Commission's Rules and Regulations §35.281(a) states that under such conditions the lease must be in writing.

7.   **a.** Pennsylvania Landlord and Tenant Act §250.511a(a) states that under the conditions referred to in the question, a maximum security deposit of one-month's rent may be required.

8.   **c.** Neither a nor b is false. Under the Pennsylvania Uniform Partnership Act and under the Pennsylvania Revised Uniform Limited Partnership Act, both general and limited partnerships can hold title to real property in the partnership name.

9.   **c.** Pursuant to a 2014 amendment to the Pennsylvania Mechanics' Lien Law, §301(b), a subcontractor owed any amount by the general contractor who was paid in full by Bob does not have the right to a mechanics lien because the work of improvement was on a single-family home subsequently used by the owner.

10.   **d.** Chapter 56 of the Pennsylvania Consolidated Statutes permits persons other than attorneys to become an attorney-in-fact, who may, if authorized by the principal, make medical decisions on behalf of the principal.

11.   **b.** Pennsylvania does not recognize nuncupative (oral) wills.

12.   **a.** Licensees may fill in blanks in preprinted sales contracts, but may not give legal advice or write language to modify a sales agreement, which is the job of an attorney.

13.   **d.** HEMAP loan recipients are required to pay up to 35-40% of their net monthly income toward housing expense, with a minimum monthly payment to HEMAP set by law at $25.

14.   **c.** Section 35.201 of Pennsylvania's Rules and Regulations of the State Real Estate Commission defines a broker of record as the individual broker responsible for the real estate transactions of a partnership, association, or corporation that holds a broker's license.

15.   **a.** Section 455.803(f)(2) provides that the licensee's license will not be reinstated until the licensee has paid in full, *plus interest at the rate of 10% a year*, the amount paid from the Real Estate Recovery Fund.

16.   **a.** Section 35.325(a)(3) of the Rules and Regulations of the State Real Estate Commission states that such an escrow account must provide for the withdrawal of funds without prior notice.

17.   **b.** Pennsylvania permits a broker to designate one salesperson to represent the seller and another salesperson to represent the buyer. In such a situation of designated agency, the broker is a dual agent owing fiduciary duties to both the buyer and to the seller, but the designated salespersons only owe fiduciary duties to the party to whom they have been designated to represent. In other words, in Pennsylvania designated agency is an exception to general agency law holding that a licensee employed by a broker owes the same duties to the principal as does the broker.

18.   **a.** Section 35.332(c) of Pennsylvania's Rules and Regulations of the State Real Estate Commission states that only choice a is correct.

19.   **a.** The Seller's Property Disclosure Statement contained in Section 35.335a of Pennsylvania's Rules and Regulations of the State Real Estate Commission states that the fact that a structural element, system or subsystem is near, at or beyond the end of its normal useful life is *not* by itself a material defect.

20.   **b.** Section 455.608 of Pennsylvania's Real Estate Licensing and Regulation Act (RELRA) provides that a Consumer Notice must be presented to a potential seller or buyer at the initial interview.

21.   **a.** Section 455.604(12) of Pennsylvania's Real Estate Licensing and Registration Act (RELRA) states that accepting a commission or any valuable consideration by a salesperson or associate broker for the performance of any acts requiring a real estate license is prohibited except from the licensed real estate broker with whom the salesperson or associate broker is affiliated.

22.   **c.** Pennsylvania law provides for transaction licensee status, under which a licensee must be a licensed salesperson or broker but does *not* act as an agent of either party and does not owe a fiduciary duty to either party. *See*, §455.201 of Pennsylvania's Real Estate Licensing and Registration Act (RELRA).

23.   **c.** Kathy and Mary owe fiduciary duties to the seller and to the buyer, respectively, not the other way around. Although some states that permit designated agency do not see the broker as a dual agent if the broker remains totally uninvolved in the transaction, Section 35.315(e)(4) of Pennsylvania's Rules and Regulations of the State Real Estate Commission provides that the broker is a dual agent and must be disclosed as such to the parties to the transaction.

24.   **b.** Rental listing referral agents and campground membership salespersons have education requirements, but building-owner salespersons do not, though they must pass the standard real estate salesperson license exam. *See*, RELRA §455.551.

25.   **d.** A broker-owner salesperson licensee must be at least *18 years of age* (RELRA §455.551) and be able to demonstrate a good reputation for honesty, integrity, etc. (RELRA §455.501), but does not need to satisfy any education requirement.

26.   **b.** Pursuant to RELRA §455.702(a), no violation of any of the provisions of the RELRA on the part of any salesperson, associate broker, or other employee of any licensed broker, shall be grounds for the revocation or suspension of the license of the employer of such salesperson, associate broker, or employee, unless it shall appear upon the hearings held, that such employer had *actual* knowledge of such violation.

27.   **d.** Pursuant to Pennsylvania Rules and Regulations of the Real estate Commission §245(a), a salesperson's license must be displayed in the employing broker's main office.

28.   **a.** Pursuant to RELRA §455.303, any person who is found guilty of carrying on business activities restricted to a Pennsylvania real estate licensee without having a valid license may, after conviction of the first offense, be sentenced to pay a fine not exceeding $500 and/or to be imprisoned for not more than 3 months.

29.   **b.** Pursuant to RELRA §455.404a(e)(1), licenses may be placed on inactive status for no more than five years.

30.   **c.** Pursuant to RELRA §455.302, Emily cannot bring any action for any service for which a real estate license is required.

31.   **d.** Land, appurtenances, and things affixed to the land are the three broad categories of real property.

32.   **a.** Property taxes are the main source of revenue for most local governments. The federal government does not tax land.

33.   **b.** Utility (also referred to as functional utility) refers to the usefulness of property — its ability to satisfy a potential buyer's need or desire, such as to provide shelter or income.

34.   **d.** A high LTV is perceived as a high risk by lenders.

35.   **c.** A special agent is an agent for a particular act or transaction.

36.   **d.** In many states, the seller of a residential property consisting of 1 to 4 dwelling units is responsible for filling out a property condition disclosure statement.

37.   **b.** In regard to the extent of performance, a contract may be executory or executed. An executed contract is a contract that has been fully performed. An executory contract is one in which some performance by one or both parties remains to be done.

38.   **c.** A title search is an examination of all relevant public documents to determine whether there exist any potential defects (such as judicial liens, lis pendens, or other encumbrances, including tax liens and special assessments) against the title.

39.   **b.** Examples of non-trust funds include a broker's real estate commissions, rent and security deposits from a broker's own real estate, and any other funds personally owned by a broker.

40.   **c.** The zoning regulations require that the depth of the lot (125') be reduced by 15 ' + 10' = 25' and that the length of the lot (160') be reduced by 10' + 10' = 20'. Therefore, the dimensions of the buildable area of the lot are 100' × 140'.

41.   **c.** Under the Interstate Land Sales Full Disclosure Act, a developer must provide each prospective buyer with a Property Report that contains pertinent information about the subdivision and that discloses to the prospective buyer that he or she has a minimum of 7 days in which to rescind the purchase agreement.

42.   **c.** One of the three broad categories of real property is "things affixed to the land."

43.   **b.** One should be careful to distinguish eminent domain, for which just compensation must be made, from police power, which is the power of a government to impose restrictions on private rights, including property rights, for the sake of public welfare, health, order, and security, for which no compensation need be made. Examples of the use of police power in regard to real property include the creation and enforcement of zoning codes, building codes, subdivision regulations, and property setbacks.

44.   **b.** Appraised value is of the value placed on a property by an appraiser, and is usually intended to estimate the market value of the property.

45.   **c.** The Homeowner's Protection Act requires that PMI be canceled when the mortgage balance reaches 78% of the property value (77% for "high risk loans") and the borrower is current on the loan.

46.   **b.** A transactional broker does not owe fiduciary duties to either party and is therefore not held to the same legal standards of conduct as is a licensed real estate agent. However, the states that permit this kind of nonagent status impose an obligation on the nonagent to act fairly, honestly, and competently to find qualified buyers or suitable properties.

47.   **b.** Many states require an agent to perform due diligence to investigate the property to ensure that the property is as represented by the seller and to disclose accurate and complete information regarding the property to potential purchasers.

48.   **a.** Consent that is not freely given, such as consent obtained by duress, menace, fraud, or undue influence, is consent that may be rescinded by the party defrauded.

49.   **b.** A contingency clause is a contract provision that makes performance of a certain act conditional on the occurrence of a specified event.

50.   **c.** *Shelley v. Kraemer* held that private, racially-based restrictive covenants are invalid under the Fourteenth Amendment.

51.   **a.** Loan amount = $275,000 × .8 = $220,000.
Down payment = purchase price - loan amount = $280,000 - $220,000 = $60,000.

52.   **a.** Situs refers to both the legal location of something and to the preference for a particular location.

53.   **a.** Inverse condemnation is an action brought by property owners.

54.   **c.** The EPA defines brownfields as "real property, the expansion, redevelopment, or reuse of which may be complicated by the presence or potential presence of a hazardous substance, pollutant, or contaminant."

55.   **b.** The process of gathering together two or more parcels to make the whole more valuable than the sum of its parts is called assemblage.

56.   **b.** Replacement cost or summation approach obtains the market value of the subject property by adding the value of the land (unimproved) of the subject property to the depreciated value of the cost (if purchased at current prices) of the improvements on the subject property.

57.   **b.** Under an adjustable-rate mortgage, the benchmark rate of interest that is adjusted periodically is referred to as the index.

58.   **d.** A homeowner with a reverse mortgage continues to be responsible for paying property taxes; paying homeowners insurance premiums; paying any homeowners association assessment fees; and maintaining the home in good repair.

59.   **b.** An agency relationship created by a verbal agreement is created by express agreement. Not all agency relationships need to be in writing.

60.   **d.** A universal agent is an agent given power of attorney to act on behalf of a principal for an unlimited range of legal matters.

61.   **c.** We both promised something, making the contract bilateral. Until both parties fulfill their promise the contract remains executory.

62.   **b.** A net listing is a listing agreement that provides a broker with all proceeds received from a sale over a specified amount.

63.   **b.** A lease constitutes an executory bilateral contract between landlord and tenant that governs such matters as the landlord's maintenance of the property and the tenant's duty to make lease payments. This contract aspect of a lease creates privity of contract between landlord and tenant.

64.   **c.** The statute of frauds is a law that requires certain types of contracts, including most real estate contracts, to be in writing and signed by the party to be bound in order for the contract to be enforceable.

65.   **a.** Under a gross lease, the tenant pays a fixed rental amount, and the landlord pays all of the operating expenses for the premises.

66.   **c.** A holder of a mortgage or deed of trust with a power-of-sale clause may, if so desired, use judicial foreclosure; however, many states have a one-action rule, under which a choice of either judicial or non-judicial foreclosure must be made.

67.   **a.** The Federal Fair Housing Act does not limit the applicability of any reasonable local, State or Federal restrictions regarding the maximum number of occupants permitted to occupy a dwelling.

68.   **d.** A real estate agency is generally considered to be a single entity for antitrust purposes, and one of the requirements to find a price-fixing, market allocation, or group boycott antitrust violation is that there existed an agreement between two or more persons.

69.   **c.** $172,367 × .04 ÷ 12 = $574.56 (first month's interest)
$1,275 - $574.56 = $700.44 (first month's principal payment)
$172,367 - $700.44 = $171,666.56 (principal balance after first month's payment).

70.   **c.** Homeowners insurance premiums, FHA mortgage insurance premiums, and private mortgage insurance premiums are *not* deductible.

71.   **c.** An easement is a non-possessory right to use a portion of another property owner's land for a specific purpose.

72.   **c.** As asbestos ages, it breaks down to small fibers that, if inhaled in sufficient quantity over sufficient time, can cause a variety of ailments, including a type of cancer known as mesothelioma.

73.   **a.** Conditional use refers to an exception for special uses such as for churches, schools, and hospitals that wish to locate to areas zoned exclusively for residential use.

74. **d.** The market or sales comparison approach (also known as the market data approach) is the best method for appraising land, residences, and other properties for which there is a ready market of similar properties.

75. **d.** One of the disadvantages of an FHA-insured loan is that properties must meet certain minimum standards as determined by an FHA-approved appraiser.

76. **c.** A buyer's agent who is a dual agent owes fiduciary duties to both the buyer and the seller.

77. **d.** A broker's principal is also referred to as the broker's client.

78. **d.** The person whose property is listed by a broker is referred to as the seller, the client, or the principal; the buyer is the customer.

79. **c.** Megan's law is an informal name for various federal and state laws that provide for the registration of sex offenders and for the making available to the public information regarding the location of these offenders.

80. **b.** The EPA pamphlet Protect Your Family From Lead In Your Home must be given to tenants as well as to buyers.

81. **b.** Under a net lease, the tenant pays a fixed rental amount plus some of the landlord's operating expenses (such as a percent of property taxes).

82. **c.** A lease with an obligation to purchase (also referred to as a lease-purchase) is typically used when the tenant-buyer wants to purchase a property but does not yet have the down payment or other ability to purchase the property at the present. Typically, a lease-purchase will provide that a portion of each rental payment will be applied to the purchase price, so that at some point the remaining amount necessary to complete the purchase is within the tenant's ability to do so.

83. **c.** Privity of contract is a legal doctrine that states that a legally enforceable relationship exists between the persons who are parties to a contract.

84. **c.** The IRS requires escrow agents to report every sale of real estate on Form 1099-S, giving the seller's name, Social Security number, and the gross sale proceeds.

85. **d.** The Federal Fair Housing Act prohibits discriminatory access to multiple listing services.

86. **b.** Placing a number on the Do-Not-Call Registry prohibits commercial calls from persons with whom the receivers of the calls have no established business relationship.

87. **d.** Comparable 1: 100' × 110' = 11,000 sq. ft.
$99,000 ÷ 11,000 sq. ft. = $9/sq. ft.
Comparable 2: 120' × 130' = 15,600 sq. ft.
$132,600 ÷ 15,600 sq. ft. = $8.50/sq. ft.
Comparable 3: 110' × 130' = 14,300 sq. ft.
$135,850 ÷ 14,300 sq. ft. = $9.5/sq. ft.
($9 + $8.5 + $9.5) ÷ 3 comparables = $9/sq. ft.
Estimated value of subject property: 110' × 140'= 15,400 sq. ft.
15,400 sq. ft. × $9/sq. ft. = $138,600.

88. **d.** Special assessment liens are encumbrances against properties in a particular area that are benefited by improvements such as for streets, water, and sewers.

89. **a.** The primary characteristic of an estate is its duration.

90.   **b.** A covenant is a promise placed in a deed, stating that the owner will do something (an affirmative covenant, such a promise to maintain a party wall) or not do something (a negative covenant, such as a promise not to build a fence). Remedies for breach of a covenant are either monetary or injunctive relief.

21.   **b.** Loss in value due to wear and tear of use is referred to as physical obsolescence.

92.   **b.** The capitalization rate for a property is calculated by dividing the annual net income by the purchase price of the property.

93.   **a.** If a broker supplies financing to remodel a condo with the stipulation that the broker will have the listing to sell the condo, the broker's agency is coupled with an interest.

94.   **c.** The transfer by will of personal property is known as a bequest.

95.   **c.** A gift deed is used to convey title when no tangible consideration is given.

96.   **c.** In real estate agency, a typical case of an *impermissible* tying arrangement occurs when the sale of a property is conditioned upon the agent's obtaining the listing for future sales.

97.   **c.** Puffing is the act of expressing a positive opinion about something to induce someone to become a party to a contract.

98.   **d.** $2,970,000 × .08 = $237,600.
Annual operating expenses = $145,400 × 12 = $1,744,800.
NOI = $2,970,000 - ($237,600 + $1,744,800) = $987,600.

99.   **d.** A property's bundle of rights is all of the legal rights and privileges that attaches to ownership of property, which may include the right to possess, use, enjoy, encumber, sell, and/or exclude from others. And because these rights are created by law, they can be changed or even abolished by law — sometimes with, sometimes without, compensation.

100.   **a.** A loan under which periodic payments consist of interest only is a term loan (also referred to as a straight loan or an interest-only loan).

101.   **d.** For a VA-guaranteed loan, the appraised value of the subject property is presented in a Certificate of Reasonable Value.

102.   **c.** In any dual agency, conflicts of loyalty and confidentiality can arise, such as when, for example, the buyer wants to know whether the seller is willing to take a lower price, or conversely, when the seller wants to know whether the buyer is willing to pay a higher price. In such cases, a dual agent must not disclose price concessions from either party without the consent of the other party.

103.   **a.** A quiet title action (also referred to as a suit to quiet title) is a court proceeding intended to establish the true ownership of a property, thereby eliminating any cloud on title.

104.   **d.** To be valid, a deed must have each of the attributes described in answers a-c.

105.   **c.** Charges that in the aggregate cannot increase more than 5% is not one of the three GFE tolerance levels for settlement charges that must be included on the HUD-1 form.

106.   **b.** Procuring cause is a common law legal concept developed by the courts to determine the proportioning of commissions among agents involved in a real estate transaction.

107.   **a.** Comparable 1: $264,600 ÷ $980 = 270.

Comparable 2: $272,640 ÷ $960 = 284.
Comparable 3: $283,200 ÷ $960 = 295.
(270 + 284 + 295) ÷ 3 = 283.

108.   **d.** Judgment liens, federal income tax liens, and state income tax liens are examples of general liens.

109.   **c.** Loans under which interest rates vary over the term of the loan are adjustable-rate loans.

110.   **c.** Emily is requesting the court to order John to complete the sale; she is not requesting monetary damages. Therefore, she should seek specific performance.

PRACTICE EXAM #4:

Note: Questions 1-30 of this exam consist of *state-portion* questions of the Pennsylvania real estate exam. Questions 31-110 of this exam consist of *national-portion* questions of the Pennsylvania relics eight exam.

1. Homeowners insurance policies typically do not include coverage for

    a. wind damage

    b. mine subsidence

    c. fire damage

    d. hail damage

2. The Pennsylvania Seller Property Disclosure Statement requires disclosure of

    a. the type of sewage system for the property

    b. all appraisals obtained by the seller during the past 2 years

    c. the source of drinking water for the property

    d. both a and c

3. The process whereby property passes to the state if the owner of the property dies intestate without heirs, or if the property is abandoned, is referred to as

    a. attachment

    b. reversion

    c. escheat

    d. Eminent domain

4. Joyce conveys her condo to her brother John on conditioned that he obtains a master's degree in physics within 5 years. John receives a

    a. fee simple absolute

    b. fee simple determinable

    c. fee simple subject to a condition subsequent

    d. life estate

5. in Pennsylvania, for how many years must a person make use of another's land to acquire an easement by prescription?

    a. 5

    b. 10

    c. 15

144

d. 21

6. In Pennsylvania, if a real estate licensee is not involved in transacting a lease between a landlord and tenant, the maximum term of an enforceable oral lease is

a. 1 year

b. 2 years

c. 3 years

d. 4 years

7. In Pennsylvania, during the first year of any residential lease, what is the maximum amount a landlord may require as security for payment of damages to the leased property and/or default in rent?

a. one-month's rent

b. two-month's rent

c. three-month's rent

d. six-month's rent

8. Under Pennsylvania law, which of the following is (are) false?

a. A conveyance of real property to a husband and wife is presumed to create a tenancy by the entireties.

b. Only a husband and wife can be tenants by the entireties.

c. Both a and b.

d. Neither a nor b.

9. To file a mechanics' Lien in Pennsylvania, a claim must be for an amount that is in excess of

a. $1,000

b. $500

c. $250

d. $100

10. Which, if any, of the following licensees may file a commercial real estate broker lien in regard to a Pennsylvania commercial real estate transaction?

a. A broker employed by another broker

b. A salesperson

c. Neither a nor b

d. Both a and b

11. Under Pennsylvania law

a. an acknowledgment is not necessary to render a deed valid between the grantor and the grantee

b. an acknowledgment is necessary to render a deed valid between the grantor and the grantee

c. and unacknowledged deed is valid against any person who is chargeable with actual notice

d. both a and c

12. Under Pennsylvania law, which, if any, of the following statements is false?

a. The statute of limitations period for written contracts is 4 years.

b. The statute of limitations period for oral contracts is 2 years.

c. The Discovery Rule permits the tolling of the statute of limitations under certain circumstances.

d. None of the above.

13. Under Pennsylvania law, which of the following statements is true?

a. Prepayment penalties may be charged on residential mortgages of $30,000 or less.

b. Prepayment penalties may be charged on residential mortgages of $40,000 or less.

c. Prepayment penalties may be charged on residential mortgages of $200,000 or less.

d. None of the above is true.

14. The maximum rate of interest that can be charged under Pennsylvania's usury law for residential mortgages insured by the FHA is

a. the maximum rate, if any, prescribed by the FHA or other law

b. 6 %

c. 4%

d. 2 %

15. Susan is a Pennsylvania salesperson employed by broker Margaret. Ted is a broker who cooperates with Margaret to sell an expensive luxury home. The sale transaction was handled primarily by Susan. Ted was very impressed and appreciative of Susan's work and offers to give her a $1,000 bonus. From the following, which is the better, more complete statement?

a. Susan may not accept Ted's offer.

b. Susan may accept Ted's offer if Margaret gives her verbal approval.

c. Susan may accept Ted's offer if Margaret gives her written approval.

d. Susan may accept Ted's offer without receiving any consent from Margaret because Ted was a cooperating broker working with Margaret on the transaction.

16. With few exceptions, a broker or cemetery broker must retain records pertaining to a real estate transaction for at least how many years following consummation of the transaction?

 a. 5

 b. 3

 c. 2

 d. 1

17. In Pennsylvania

 a. a designated agent is a licensee designated by the employing broker, with the consent of the principal, to act exclusively as an agent on behalf of the principal to the exclusion of all other licensees within the broker's employ.

 b. the employing broker of designated agents is not considered to be a dual agent as long as the broker remains totally uninvolved in the transaction

 c. both a and c

 d. either a nor c

18. In Pennsylvania, which, if any, of the following statements is (are) true?

 a. A licensee who sells his or her *own* real estate, does not need to inform the purchaser that the licensee is a real estate licensee.

 b. A transaction licensee does not owe fiduciary duties to either party to a real estate transaction.

 c. Both a and b are true.

 d. Neither a nor b is true.

19. In Pennsylvania, for the purchase or sale of residential or commercial real estate or for the lease of residential or commercial real estate when the licensee is working on behalf of the tenant, licensees must provide which of the following to the consumer at the initial interview?

 a. Purchase/lease agreement

 b. Escrow instructions

 c. Seller's/landlord's disclosure statement

 d. Consumer Notice

20. Under Pennsylvania's Real Estate Seller Disclosure Act, which of the following statements is (are) false?

 a. A seller of residential property must, with a few exceptions, disclose to the buyer all material defects if the property consists of 1-5 dwelling units.

 b. A material defect is a problem with a residential real property or any portion of it that would have a significant adverse impact on the value of the property or that involves an unreasonable risk to people on the property.

c. Both a and b are false.

d. Neither a nor b is false.

21. Pennsylvania's Plain Language Consumer Contract Act applies to

　a. an individual who leases an apartment

　b. real estate deeds

　c. title insurance contracts

　d. both a and b

22. Margaret is a broker who worked with Julie and Ted, who are salesperson's employed by broker Emily, who cooperated with Margaret in the sale of a luxury home. Julie and Ted were designated agents representing the seller and the buyer, respectively, in the transaction.

　a. Margaret may pay part of the commission she earned from this transaction to Julie.

　b. Margaret may pay part of the commission she earned from this transaction to Ted.

　c. Margaret may pay part of the commission she earned from this transaction to both Julie and Ted.

　d. Margaret may pay part of the commission she earned from this transaction to neither Julie nor Ted.

23. Mark is a broker who employs both Keri and Millie as salespersons. Mark designates Keri as a designated agent for the seller and Millie as a designated agent for the buyer in regard to the sale of a home. Under Pennsylvania law,

　a. Keri owes fiduciary duties to the buyer.

　b. Millie owes fiduciary duties to the seller.

　c. Mark owes fiduciary duties to both the seller and to the buyer.

　d. Mark does not owe fiduciary duties to the seller and to the buyer.

24. Ron lists his home as for sale by owner. Steve is interested in purchasing Ron's home but would like to have a broker assist in seeing to it that all of the paperwork necessary to complete the transaction is properly prepared. Ron and the Steve therefore approach broker Emily and ask her for assistance. In Pennsylvania, which, if any, of the following statements is (are) true?

　a. Emily must represent both Ron and Steve as a dual agent.

　b. Emily would be permitted to act as a dual agent if both Ron and Steve are so informed and agree in writing.

　c. Emily may act as a transaction licensee.

　d. Both b and c are true statements.

25. In Pennsylvania, an individual who applies for a broker license need not

　a. be at least 21 years of age

b. complete at least 250 hours in real estate education

c. have been engaged as a licensed real estate salesperson for at least three years or possess educational or experience qualifications which the commission deems to be the equivalent thereof

d. pass the broker license exam

26. In Pennsylvania, an associate broker or salesperson may hold deposits or other escrow under what conditions?

a. Only upon given written permission by the person who gives over the deposit or other escrow.

b. Only upon given written permission by all parties to the transaction.

c. Only if the amount of the deposit or other escrow is valued at under $100.

d. An associate broker or salesperson may not hold deposits or other escrow.

27. If one has not been actively licensed as a broker or salesperson in another state, within how many years must one submit a properly completed license application to become a Pennsylvania salesperson after receiving a passing score on each part of the salesperson's licensing examination?

a. 5 years

b. 4 years

c. 3 years

d. 1 year

28. Myra is a Pennsylvania real estate salesperson whose license was revoked because she accepted compensation directly from a client who was pleased with her work. Myra may petition the Commission for relicensure

a. never

b. 5 years after revocation of her license

c. 4 years after revocation of her license

d. 1 year after revocation of her license

29. A licensee who was issued a license more than 6 months prior to the end of the biennial license period must complete how many hours of Commission-approved continuing education during that that initial license period to renew the licensee's license?

a. 16 hours

b. 14 hours

c. 12 hours

d. 6 hours

30. Members of the Pennsylvania Real Estate Commission are selected by

a the Pennsylvania Department of Commerce

b the Governor

c a special selection committee of Realtors®

d the Pennsylvania Bureau of Consumer Affairs

31. Sally dismantled her pergola, stacking the lumber in a corner of her backyard. The lumber became personal property through an act of

a. annexation

b. heterogeneity

c. severance

d. fixity

32. In most states, certain kinds of property owners are typically subject to property taxes, including

a. religious organizations

b. governmental bodies

c. educational institutions

d. single-family houses

33. Township A and township B are adjacent, with township B to the east of township A. Which section of township B is adjacent to section 12 of township A?

a. 13

b. 7

c. 18

d. 8

34. The value of a property is best described as the

a. ability to transfer some interest in the property to another

b. level of desire for a property

c. present worth to typical users or investors of all rights to future benefits, arising out of property ownership

d. lack of similar properties in the area

35. Leverage is

a. a method of hedging against recession

b. the impact on investments that results from using borrowed money to acquire the investments

c. a method used to insure against negative cash flow

d. increased by making a larger down payment

36. Most _____ are an integral part of an ongoing business enterprise, such as a branch manager who is authorized to conduct business on an ongoing basis for the branch on behalf of a company.

    a. general agents

    b. special agents

    c. designated agents

    d. specific agents

37. Pursuant to the federal Residential Lead-Based Paint Hazard Reduction Act rule, a seller (or lessor) of a residential dwelling unit built before 1978 must

    a. Fill out a property condition disclosure statement

    b. Provide a Home Warranty certificate to the purchaser before close of escrow

    c. Disclose any knowledge the seller has about whether lead-based paint was used in the dwelling unit

    d. Pay for an inspection of the property for lead-based paint

38. I promise to pay you $20 if you mow my lawn on Tuesday, and you shrug your shoulders and say, "I'll see if I have the time." If you do not mow my lawn on Tuesday, then

    a. I will owe you $20 because I did not revoke my offer.

    b. I will owe you $20 because I promised to pay you $20.

    c. I can sue you for damages because you did not mow my lawn on Tuesday and that resulted in the homeowners association fining me $100 for keeping such an unsightly front yard.

    d. I do not owe you $20, and there is no penalty to you.

39. The two main types of insurance policies are

    a. forgery coverage, defects coverage

    b. possession coverage, defects coverage

    c. standard coverage, extended coverage

    d. standard coverage, limited coverage

40. After-acquired interests are conveyed with

    a. a quitclaim deed

    b. a sheriff's deed

    c. a grant deed

    d. none of the above

41. The Federal Fair Housing Act does not prohibit

a. discrimination against children with respect to the properties where at least 80% of the dwelling units are occupied by at least one person who is 55 years of age or older

b. discriminatory advertising, sales, or loan terms

c. directing people of protected classes away from, or toward, particular areas

d. representing that prices will decline, or crime increase, or other negative effects will occur because of the entrance of minorities into particular areas

42. Alice is a salesperson with many years of experience and many former and current clients. She records a message in which she states that she has just listed 5 newly constructed homes, and sends that recorded message via an auto dialer to the cell phones of 10 clients. Alice's calls are

a. exempt from Do-Not-Call rules because she is sending the message to persons with whom she has an established business relationship

b. exempt from Do-Not-Call rules because she is sending the recorded message to fewer than 50 persons

c. exempt from Do-Not-Call rules because only calls to residential phones are restricted

d. in violation of Do-Not-Call rules because she did not receive written permission from these 10 persons before sending the prerecorded messages to their cell phones

43. José paid a 5% broker's commission and $4,600 in closing costs on the sale of his condo, which had cost him $150,000 a few years earlier. If José makes a profit of $6,900 on the sale, what was the sale price of the condo?

a. $165,158 (rounded)

b. $162,737 (rounded)

c. $157,895 (rounded)

d. none of the above

44. A 1031 exchange is

a. A tax-free exchange

b. An exchange of non-income producing personal residential property for another like-kind non-income-producing residential property

c. A tax-deferred exchange

d. A tax-accelerated exchange

45. Severance damages are associated with

a. property taxation

b. eminent domain

c. adverse possession

d. police power

46. An area near John's house has been rezoned to permit the construction of a large mall. As a result, the value of John's and his neighbors' homes have increased significantly in value. This is an example of the principle of

a. contribution

b. assemblage

c. integration

d. anticipation

47. In finance, a point is equal to

a. 1/6% of the loan amount

b. 1/8 % of the loan amount

c. 1/2% of the loan amount

d. 1% of the loan amount

48. A salesperson is a _____ of the broker's client.

a. subagent

b. single agent

c. dual agent

d. designated agent

49. Some states have gone further than to require a seller property disclosure statement by requiring

a. the listing broker to pay for a property inspection of residential properties consisting of 1 to 4 dwelling units

b. the listing broker to perform a reasonable visual inspection of residential properties consisting of 1 to 4 dwelling units

c. the seller to pay for a lead-paint inspection of residential dwelling units

d. the seller to offer a prospective buyer 3 days to inspect for lead-based paint and lead-based paint hazards

50. A lease that provides for yearly adjustments in rent based on the Consumer Price Index is called a

a. percentage lease

b. net lease

c. graduated lease

d. triple net lease

51. Evaluate the following two statements: (1) the parol evidence rule is a law that requires particular types of lawsuits to be brought within a specified time after the occurrence of the event giving rise to the lawsuit; (2) in a court action for specific performance, the amount of consideration is important.

  a. Both statements are correct.

  b. The first statement is correct and the second statement is false.

  c. The first statement is false and the second statement is true.

  d. Both statements are false.

52. A duplicate set of title records maintained at title insurance companies for use in title searches is called

  a. a title plant

  b. a chain of title

  c. an abstract of title

  d. a preliminary title report

53. Examples of trust funds do not include

  a. security deposits from a broker's own real estate

  b. funding for a client's loan

  c. interest, if any, paid in a trust fund account

  d. earnest money deposits that a prospective purchaser gives to a broker as good-faith evidence of intention to complete a transaction

54. The outstanding balance of loans against Samantha's home is $100,000. She has just arranged to obtain a home equity line of credit of 80% of the appraised value of her home, minus the total indebtedness against her home. The amount of the line of credit is $60,000. What is the appraised value of Samantha's home?

  a. $175,000

  b. $225,000

  c. $185,000

  d. none of the above

55. Appurtenances are considered

  a. personal property

  b. emblements

  c. real property

  d. trade fixtures

56. A vacant lot zoned for residential use is rezoned for commercial use. This is an example of

   a. variance

   b. conditional use

   c. spot zoning

   d. inclusionary zoning

57. The market or sales comparison approach to appraisal is based on which principle of value?

   a. principle of substitution

   b. principle of contribution

   c. principle of balance

   d. principle of supply and demand

58. Private mortgage insurance (PMI)

   a. is insurance that lenders often require for loans with an LTV more than 75%

   b. covers the top amount of a loan in case of default

   c. insures the borrower

   d. insures the trustee

59. Which of the following is not a triggering term?

   a. amount of down payment

   b. annual percentage rate

   c. amount of any payment

   d. number of payments to be made

60. Categories of stigmatized properties include

   a. properties with leaky roofs

   b. properties located in floodplains

   c. properties that have registered sex offenders living nearby

   d. properties with defective heaters

61. Broker Susan has an exclusive agency listing with John to sell his house. Before the term of Susan's listing expires, Broker Margaret sells John's house and receives the full commission from John. Susan

   a. has the right to receive half the commission from Margaret

   b. has the right to receive all of the commission from Margaret

   c. has the right to receive all of the commission from John

d. has no right to any commission from this transaction

62. To be valid, a deed need not

    a. be signed by the grantee

    b. be in writing

    c. adequately describe the property

    d. contain a granting clause

63. _____ upheld the Civil Rights Act of 1866, using the _____ as its legal basis

    a. *Jones v. Mayer*, Fourteenth Amendment

    b. *Jones v. Mayer*, Thirteenth Amendment

    c. *Shelley v. Kraemer*, Fourteenth Amendment

    d. *Shelley v. Kraemer*, Thirteenth Amendment

64. Under the Equal Credit Opportunity Act, a lender may not ask any of the following questions, except

    a. whether the applicant is married

    b. whether the applicant is divorced

    c. whether the applicant is widowed

    d. whether the applicant, if a woman of child-during age, will stop working to raise children

65. A residential property was purchased for $375,600. The state documentary transfer fee is $.75 for each $500 or fraction thereof. The property was purchased with $300,600 cash and an assumption of the $75,000 seller's mortgage. Assumed mortgages are exempt from the transfer fee in this state. What was the documentary transfer fee?

    a. $450.75

    b. $451.50

    c. $450.00

    d. $113.25

66. In general, states with ample supplies of water have adopted water rights based on

    a. prior appropriation theory

    b. riparian rights

    c. the doctrine of capture

    d. profit á prendre

67. An area of low, flat, periodically flooded land is called

a. a natural hazard

b. a negative impact area

c. an environmental hazard

d. a floodplain

68. Loss in value due to natural causes such as water damage or termites is referred to as

a. external obsolescence

b. functional obsolescence

c. economic obsolescence

d. physical obsolescence

69. One of the disadvantages of an FHA-insured loan is

a. relatively high LTVs

b. down payments can be gifted by a relative

c. upfront mortgage insurance premiums (upfront MIP) and annual MIP premiums

d. the loans cannot have a prepayment penalty

70. Amanda is involved in the sale of a condo, is not an agent for either the buyer or the seller, but owes both the buyer and the seller the obligation to act fairly, honestly, and competently toward them. Amanda likely is a

a. dual agent

b. seller's agent

c. transactional broker

d. designated agent

71. An exclusive agency listing

a. cannot take the form of a net listing

b. never needs to have a definite, specific date of termination

c. provides more security for the listing agent than does an exclusive right to sell listing

d. provides less security for the listing agent than does an exclusive right to sell listing

72. George offers to buy Emily's condo for $150,000. Emily replies that she needs at least $175,000. George replies that he is no longer interested because he has found a more suitable property. Emily, desperate to move, emails back that she will accept the $150,000. George replies that now he will only pay $130,000. George and Emily have

a. a contract to purchase the condo for $150,000

b. a contract to purchase the contract for $130,000

c. a contract to purchase the condo for $175,000

d. no contract

73. What makes the Civil Rights Act of 1866 unique is that

a. it applies only to racial and religious discrimination

b. it applies only to residential properties with more than 4 dwelling units

c. it prohibits racial discrimination in the lease or sale of all real property, commercial or residential

d. it applies only to residential properties

74. The type of nondisclosure known as concealment refers to

a. the act of expressing a positive opinion about something to induce someone to become a party to a contract

b. the act of preventing disclosure of something

c. the unauthorized misappropriation and use of another's funds or other property

d. an event that may, but is not certain to, happen, the occurrence upon which the happening of another event is dependent

75. The subject property and a comparable are homes that appear almost exactly the same except that the comparable as an inferior pool estimated to be worth $2,000 less than the subject pool, and the comparable has superior landscaping estimated to be worth $1,500 more than the subject landscaping. What adjustments should be made?

a. adjust the subject property value up by $500

b. adjust the subject property value down by $500

c. adjust the comparable property value up by $500

d. adjust the comparable property value down by $500

76. A plat is a

a. city-wide plan that addresses such issues as transportation, housing, conservation, open spaces, noise, and safety on a county- or city-wide scale

b. report containing pertinent information about the subdivision and that discloses to the prospective buyer that he or she has a minimum of 7 days in which to rescind the purchase agreement

c. detailed map showing the boundaries of the individual parcels, streets, easements, engineering data, and, often, the environmental impact of the development.

d. restriction in a deed concerning things as the height, size, and architectural styles of buildings

77. Joe has an easement appurtenant to use a walkway on Bob's property to access the beach. Joe has a

a. dominant tenement

b. easement in gross

c. license

d. specific lien

78. Under the Superfund Law, a person may be able to assert the innocent landowner defense if

a. before acquiring the property, the person undertook appropriate inquiry to ensure that the property was not contaminated

b. the person can prove that he or she is not responsible for contaminating the property

c. the person can prove that someone else contaminated the property

d. the person can prove that the site was contaminated by the prior owner or owners

79. When using the income approach to appraisal, which of the following expenses is not deducted to obtain net income?

a. maintenance costs

b. reserves for replacements of building components

c. mortgage payments

d. hazard insurance

80. Which of the following are not included in PITI calculations?

a. private mortgage insurance

b. real estate taxes

c. car payments

d. homeowner's insurance

81. A real estate broker owes a special relationship of _____, _____, and _____ to the broker's clients.

a. care, honesty, general agency

b. loyalty, universality, honesty

c. loyalty, trust, care

d. trust, honesty, ratification

82. Natural Hazards Areas include

a. flood hazard areas

b. fire hazard areas

c. earthquake zones

d. all of the above

83. An implied contract is

a. a contract that has not yet been fully performed by one or both parties.

b. a contract not expressed in words, but, through action or inaction, understood by the parties.

c. a contract in which a promise given by one party is exchanged for a promise given by the other party.

d. a contract stated in words, written or oral.

84. One of the differences between a lease with an option to purchase in a lease with an obligation to purchase is that

a. the lease with an option to purchase is a unilateral contract, but the lease with an obligation to purchase is a bilateral contract.

b. the lease-purchase must be in writing, but the lease-option does not need to be in writing.

c. the lease-option must be in writing, but the lease-purchase does not need to be in writing.

d. the lease with an option to purchase gives the optionee the right but not the obligation to purchase.

85. George knowingly misrepresented the size of his house when he sold it to Susan. The purchase contract between them is

a. valid and enforceable because escrow closed

b. void from its inception

c. voidable by either George or Susan

d. voidable by Susan

86. Examples of items that an owner of his or her personal residence may deduct from his or her taxes include

a. repairs on the residence

b. loss on the sale of the residence

c. property taxes paid on the residence

d. private mortgage insurance premiums

87. A small office building generates gross monthly rentals of $3,400. It also takes in $225 per month for parking fees. The fair market value of the property is $935,000. What is the monthly gross rent multiplier for this property?

a. 258 (rounded)

b. 273 (rounded)

c. $294 (rounded)

d. none of the above

160

88. If at the end of a life estate, the future interest reverts to the grantor, the residue of the estate is called a

    a. subsequent condition

    b. remainder

    c. reversion

    d. fee simple defeasible

89. Instances of police power include

    a. inverse condemnation

    b. building codes

    c. eminent domain

    d. deed restrictions

90. When the three appraisal approaches give different valuations, an appraiser will arrive at a final estimate by the use of

    a. value correction

    b. adjustment

    c. averaging the valuations

    d. reconciliation

91. Which of the following statements is false?

    a. Under an adjustable-rate mortgage, the benchmark rate of interest that is adjusted periodically according to the going rate of T-bills, LIBOR, or the like is referred to as the index

    b. Margin is a number of percentage points, usually fixed over the life of the loan, that is added to the index of an adjustable-rate mortgage to arrive at the fully indexed rate.

    c. In adjustable-rate mortgage, the fully indexed rate = index - margin.

    d. The discounted rate is a rate (also called a teaser rate) on an adjustable-rate mortgage that is less than the fully indexed rate.

92. When a principal intentionally, or by want of ordinary care, causes a third person to believe another to be his agent who is not actually employed by the principal, _____ is created.

    a. an agency by ratification

    b. a universal agency

    c. an ostensible agency

    d. a designated agency

93. Most states require a listing agent to disclose the agency relationship to the seller

    a. before escrow closes

    b. as soon as all contingencies have been met

    c. before the seller signs the listing agreement

    d. before the buyer signs the purchase agreement

94. A contract that was valid at its inception may become _____ after a certain passage of time due to _____.

    a. unenforceable, the statute of limitations

    b. unenforceable, the statute of frauds

    c. void, the statute of limitations

    d. void, the statute of frauds

95. Which of the following statements is false?

    a. An assignment typically relieves the assignor of all liability under the contract.

    b. A contract can be discharged by being fully performed.

    c. A breach is a failure to perform in accordance with the terms of a contract.

    d. Rescission extinguishes a contract and returns each party to the position it was in immediately prior to the formation of the contract.

96. In order for an antitrust conspiracy to occur, how many persons must agree to act in a manner that has the effect of restraining trade?

    a. 1

    b. 2

    c. 3

    d. 4

97. Alan and Susan's combined monthly gross income is $6,000. If a lender requires a PITI of 32%, what is the maximum PITI with which Alan and Susan can qualify?

    a. $4,080

    b. $1,920

    c. $1,800

    d. none of the above

98. All of the legal rights and privileges that attaches to ownership of property is referred to as

    a. a freehold estate

    b. natural rights

c. bundle of rights

d. a life estate

99. John's new house was built to close to the street, violating a zoning ordinance relating to setbacks. John should apply for a

a. nonconforming use

b. variance

c. spot zoning

d. conditional use

100. The secondary mortgage market is

a. the market created by institutions that provide mortgages subordinate to existing first mortgages on property

b. the market wherein mortgages are sold by primary mortgage lenders to investors, such as pension funds and insurance companies

c. the market created especially for nonconforming loans

d. the market in which conforming loans are created

101. Which of the following statements is true?

a. Typically, real estate law requires that a licensee who is acting *solely* as a principal in a real estate transaction must reveal his or her status as a licensee.

b. A conflict of interest can only exist if there is actual undue influence.

c. Conversion is the act of improperly segregating the funds belonging to the agent from the funds received and held on behalf of another.

d. Real estate law typically does not require that a licensee who is acting *solely* as a principal in a real estate transaction must reveal his or her status as a licensee.

102. An agency is _____ if the agent has a financial interest in the subject of the agency.

a. coupled with an interest

b. a designated agency

c. an implied agency

d. a ratified agency

103. A contract provision stating that no prior agreement or contemporaneous oral agreement will have any force or effect is called

a. a severability clause

b. an ironclad merger clause

c. a contingency clause

d. a safety clause

104. A good-faith estimate (GFE) of all fees and costs related to closing a loan on a federally insured home must be provided to a potential borrower within how many days after submission of a mortgage loan application?

    a. 21 days

    b. 15 days

    c. 10 days

    d. 3 days

105. Which of the following statements is true?

    a. An MLS may refuse membership to a broker who discounts fees beyond a certain point.

    b. A broker may not offer a competing broker a referral fee.

    c. Competing brokers may receive compensation from both the buyer and the seller in the same transaction.

    d. A broker may not discuss with a cooperating broker how to split a commission fee when negotiating a particular transaction.

106. An official charge against property as security for the payment of a debt or an obligation owed for services rendered is

    a. a lien

    b. an encroachment

    c. a support right

    d. a profit á prendre

107. Which of the following is true?

    a. a CMA is not prepared by brokers

    b. a CMA never considers currently listed properties

    c. a CMA never considers properties whose listings have expired

    d. a market data appraisal does not consider properties that have not sold

108. The person who receives real property by will is known as

    a. a devisee

    b. a legatee

    c. an heir

    d. a grantee

109. Which of the following statements is false?

    a. All real estate agency compensation is subject to negotiation.

b. The source of a real estate agent's compensation does not determine agency representation.

c. A few states do not require brokers to inform parties to a real estate transaction as to whom the broker is representing.

d. A conflict of interest is a situation in which an individual or organization is involved in several *potentially* competing interests, creating a risk that one interest *might* unduly influence another interest.

110. Emily sells her house, giving a deed that warrants that she owns the property, has the right to convey it, and that the property was not encumbered during the period of time that she owned the house. Emily gave what type of deed?

a. quitclaim deed

b. grant deed

c. special warranty deed

d. general warranty deed

ANSWERS TO PRACTICE EXAM #4:

Note: If you would like to obtain a deeper understanding of the real estate principles behind the answers to the ***national*** portion of the exam, please consult the supplemental textbook *PSI Real Estate Exam Prep 2015-2016*, which provides a thorough, up-to-date review of the real estate principles covered in the ***national*** portion of the Pennsylvania real estate exam. This textbook is available both in print and Kindle formats on Amazon.com.

1.   **b.** Mine subsidence is not typically included in homeowners insurance policies; however, special mine subsidence insurance is available. In 1961, Pennsylvania established the Mine Subsidence Insurance Fund to provide insurance against losses caused by mine subsidence.

2.   **d.** The Seller Property Disclosure Statement, Section 8(i), asks "What is the source of your drinking water?" and Section 8(iv) asks "What is the type of sewage system?"

3.   **c.** Pennsylvania's Commonwealth Unclaimed Property Law governs the process of escheat of real and personal property.

4.   **c.** Pennsylvania has adopted the two common law categories of fee simple defeasible estates: fee simple determinable and fee simple subject to a condition subsequent. A fee simple determinable is an estate that automatically reverts to the grantor upon the occurrence of a specified event with no need to take court action. A fee simple subject to a condition subsequent is an estate that, upon the noncompliance of the stated condition, the grantor or the grantor's successors in interest would have the right to terminate the preceding estate but must take court action to assert the right of termination and reversion. "On condition" is considered a limitation imposing a condition subsequent.

5.   **d.** To acquire a prescriptive easement in Pennsylvania, one must have used on a continuous, exclusive, adverse, notorious, and open basis another's land for 21 years.

6.   **c.** Section 250.201 of the Pennsylvania Landlord and Tenant Act states that an oral lease for a period of 3 years or less may be oral. Note, however, that, as a general rule, if a licensee is involved in the transaction, the lease must be in writing. For exceptions, see Real Estate Commissioner's Rules and Regulations §35.281(b).

7.   **b.** Pennsylvania Landlord and Tenant Act §250.511a(a) states that under the conditions referred to in the question, a maximum security deposit of two-month's rent may be required.

8.   **d.** Neither a nor b is false, i.e, they are both true statements of Pennsylvania law. *Be careful with questions containing the word "false."*

9.   **b.** A claim for a mechanics' Lien must exceed $500. Pennsylvania Mechanics' Lien Law §301(a).

10.   **c.** The Pennsylvania Commercial Real Estate Broker Lien Act permits a commercial real estate broker lien to be recorded by a broker involved in the commercial real estate transaction, but not by associate brokers or salespersons

11.   **d.** Under Pennsylvania law, and unacknowledged deed is valid between the parties to the deed and to all others who are chargeable with actual notice. An unacknowledged deed does not, however, provide constructive notice to the public.

12.   **b.** The Pennsylvania statute of limitations period for written and oral contracts is 4 years. A typical case in which the Discovery Rule is involved is in a fraud case where the fraud (which by its nature is deceptive) was not discovered for some time after the fraud took place.

13.   **d.** In 2007, Pennsylvania adjusted its ban on prepayment penalties on residential loans from $50,000 or less to $217,873 or less, an amount to be adjusted yearly for inflation.

14.   **a.** Pennsylvania usury law does not set a maximum interest rate on residential mortgages insured or guaranteed, in whole or in part, by the FHA, the VA, or other U.S. government departments or agencies.

15.   **a.** Section 455.604(12) of Pennsylvania's Real Estate Licensing and Registration Act (RELRA) states that accepting a commission or any valuable consideration by a salesperson or associate broker for the performance of any acts requiring a real estate license is prohibited except from the licensed real estate broker with whom the salesperson or associate broker is affiliated.

16.   **b.** Section 35.286 of the Pennsylvania Code (Standards of Conduct and Practice) provides that, with a few exceptions, a broker or cemetery broker must retain records pertaining to a real estate transaction for at least 3 years following consummation of the transaction.

17.   **a.** Although some states that permit designated agency do not see the broker as a dual agent if the broker remains totally uninvolved in the transaction, Section 35.315(e)(4) of Pennsylvania's Rules and Regulations of the State Real Estate Commission provides that the broker is a dual agent and must be disclosed as such to the parties to the transaction.

18.   **b.** Answer a is false because section 35.288 of Pennsylvania's Rules and Regulations of the State Real Estate Commission provides that a licensee who sells his or her own real estate must inform the purchaser that the licensee is a real estate licensee. Additionally, answer b is true because Pennsylvania law provides for transaction licensee status, under which a licensee does not act as an agent of either party and does not owe a fiduciary duty to either party. *See*, §455.201 of Pennsylvania's Real Estate Licensing and Registration Act (RELRA).

19.   **d.** Section 35.336 of Pennsylvania's Rules and Regulations of the State Real Estate Commission provides that for the purchase or sale of residential or commercial real estate or for the lease of residential or commercial real estate when the licensee is working on behalf of the tenant, the licensee must provide the consumer with the Consumer Notice at their initial interview.

20.   **a.** Pennsylvania's Real Estate Seller Disclosure Act applies with a few stated exceptions (*see*, §7302) to transfers of all residential property, where the term "residential real estate transfer" is defined to mean a transfer of any interest in real property that consists of not less than one nor more than *four* residential dwelling units, whether by sale, exchange, installment sales contract, lease with an option to purchase, grant or transfer of unit in a residential condominium or cooperative.

21.   **a.** Exclusions to Pennsylvania's Plain Language Consumer Contract Act (§2204(b)) include real estate deeds and the title insurance contracts.

22.   **d.** Section 455.604(12.1) of Pennsylvania's Real Estate Licensing and Registration Act (RELRA) states that the paying of a commission or any valuable consideration by a broker to anyone other than his or her licensed employees or another real estate broker for any act requiring a real estate license is prohibited.

23.   **c.** Although some states that permit designated agency do not see the broker as a dual agent if the broker remains totally uninvolved in the transaction, Section 35.315(e)(4) of Pennsylvania's Rules and Regulations of the State Real Estate Commission provides that the broker is a dual agent and must be disclosed as such to the parties to the transaction.

24.   **d.** Under Pennsylvania law, Emily may act as a transaction licensee if she avoids representing either Ron or Steve as an agent; i.e., she lets them do the negotiating between themselves and she merely facilitates the transaction by seeing to it that the proper procedures and paperwork are completed. Of course, Emily would also be permitted to act as a dual agent if Ron and Steve are properly informed and so agree in writing.

25.   **b.** The education requirement for a broker license is contained in RELRA §455.511(2): "The applicant shall have completed 240 hours in real estate instruction in areas of study prescribed by the rules of the commission, which rules shall require instruction in the areas of fair housing and professional ethics.

26.   **d.** Pursuant to RELRA §455.608e(c), every associate broker or salesperson shall, promptly following receipt of a deposit or other escrow, pay over the funds to the broker employing the associate broker or salesperson.

27.   **c.** Pursuant to Pennsylvania Rules and Regulations of the Real Estate Commission §223(a) (1), a potential salesperson licensee must have scored a passing grade on each part of the salesperson's licensing examination within 3 years prior to the submission of a properly completed license application, except that an applicant who has been actively licensed as a broker or a salesperson by another state within the last 5 years shall take and pass only the Pennsylvania portion of the examination.

28.   **b.** Pursuant to Pennsylvania Rules and Regulations of the Real Estate Commission §251, the Commission will not authorize relicensure of an individual whose license has been revoked for at least 5 years following the date revocation begins. After the 5-year period, the individual may petition the Commission for relicensure. The decision to permit relicensure is within the Commission's discretion. If relicensure is permitted, the individual must comply with current requirements for licensure before the license is issued.

29.   **b.** Pursuant to Pennsylvania Rules and Regulations of the State Real Estate Commission §382(b), a broker or salesperson holding a standard license who desires to reactivate and renew a noncurrent license shall, as a condition precedent to reactivation and renewal, complete 14 hours of Commission-approved continuing education during the 2-year period preceding the date of submission of the reactivation application. However, pursuant to §383(a)(1), a standard license holder who seeks to renew a current license that was initially issued within 6 months of the biennial license period for which renewal is sought will be deemed eligible, on the basis of hardship, for a full waiver of the continuing education requirement.

30.   **b.** Pursuant to RELRA §202(a) each member of the Commission is appointed by the Governor.

31.   **c.** Severance is the act of detaching an item from real property that changes the item to personal property.

32.   **d.** Religious organizations, governmental bodies, and educational institutions, are typically not subject to property tax.

33.   **b.** See diagram below.

A theoretical township showing numbered sections (large bold type) and adjacent township sections (smaller regular type).							
36	31	32	33	34	35	36	31
1	**6**	**5**	**4**	**3**	**2**	**1**	6
12	**7**	**8**	**9**	**10**	**11**	**12**	7
13	**18**	**17**	**16**	**15**	**14**	**13**	18
24	**19**	**20**	**21**	**22**	**23**	**24**	19
25	**30**	**29**	**28**	**27**	**26**	**25**	30
36	**31**	**32**	**33**	**34**	**35**	**36**	31
1	6	5	4	3	2	1	6

34.   **c.** The value of a property is best described as the present worth to typical users or investors of all rights to future benefits, arising out of property ownership.

35.   **b.** Leverage results in multiplying gains (or losses) on investments by using borrowed money to acquire the investments.

36.   **a.** Most general agents are an integral part of an ongoing business enterprise, such as a branch manager who is authorized to conduct business on an ongoing basis for the branch on behalf of a company.

37.   **c.** Pursuant to the federal Residential Lead-Based Paint Hazard Reduction Act rule, a seller (or lessor) of a residential dwelling unit built before 1978 must notify a buyer (or tenant) in writing about required disclosures for lead-based paint.

38.   **d.** If I promise to pay you $20 if you mow my lawn on Tuesday, and you shrug your shoulders and say, "I'll see if I have time," we have a unilateral contract — you have not promised to do anything, but I have. Unless I withdraw my offer in the meanwhile, if you go ahead and mow my lawn on Tuesday, I will owe you $20. On the other hand, if you don't mow my lawn on Tuesday, there is no penalty to you, nor is there $20 owed by me to you.

39.   **c.** There are many ways in which title may be adversely affected, and, consequently, there are different policies of title insurance to cover various possible defects. The two main title insurance policies are the standard coverage and the extended coverage.

40.   **c.** A grant deed conveys all after-acquired interests in the title.

41.   **a.** The Federal Fair Housing Act does not prohibit discrimination against children with respect to the properties where at least 80% of the dwelling units are occupied by at least one person who is 55 years of age or older.

42.   **d.** Effective October 13, 2013, the FTC imposed additional Do-Not-Call rules, requiring that all sellers and telemarketers must have a consumer's written consent to make prerecorded telephone calls ("robocalls") to residential telephone numbers or auto dialed or prerecorded telemarketing calls or text messages to wireless numbers.

43.   **d.** Before the commission was paid, there was $4,600 + $150,000 + $6,900 equals $161,500 to be accounted for. Therefore, $161,500 = 95% × Sales Price. Sales Price = $161,500 ÷ .95 = $170,000.

44.   **c.** A 1031 exchange is a tax-deferred exchange (often misleadingly called a tax-free exchange) of "like kind" property held for productive use.

45.   **b.** When land is taken by eminent domain, in addition to just compensation for the value of the land taken, the owner may be able to receive severance damages if the owner's remaining land is reduced in value due to the severance of the condemned land from the owner's remaining property.

46.   **d.** The principle of anticipation states that value is derived from a calculation of anticipated future benefits to be derived from the property, not from past benefits, though past benefits may inform as to what might be expected in the future.

47.   **d.** In finance, a point is equal to 1% of the loan amount.

48.   **a.** A salesperson is a subagent of the broker's client.

49.   **b.** Some states have gone further than to require a seller property disclosure statement by requiring the listing broker to perform a reasonable visual inspection of residential properties consisting of 1 to 4 dwelling units and to disclose defects in the property, both known and discovered through this mandatory inspection, to potential purchasers before a purchase contract is signed.

50.   **c.** A graduated lease is similar to a gross lease except that it provides (in a lease provision referred to as an escalator clause) for periodic increases in the rent, often based on the Consumer Price Index.

51.   **c.** The parol evidence rule is a rule of evidence that prohibits the introduction of extrinsic evidence of preliminary negotiations, oral or written, and of contemporaneous oral evidence, to alter the terms of a written agreement that appears to be whole. In a court action for specific performance, the amount of consideration is important. Specific performance is an equitable remedy commonly sought by one party to a real estate contract seeking a court order requiring the other party to perform what was specifically stated in the contract (such as transferring the deed to the property), as an alternative to awarding damages. As a general rule, to obtain an equitable remedy (as opposed to a legal remedy of monetary damages), the fairness or adequacy of consideration will weigh heavily in the court's deliberations.

52.   **a.** A title plant is a set of title records maintained at title insurance companies for use in title searches.

53.   **a.** Examples of non-trust funds include a broker's real estate commissions, rent and security deposits from a broker's own real estate, and any other funds personally owned by a broker.

54.   **d.** (appraised value × .8) - $100,000 = $60,000. Therefore, appraised value = $160,000 ÷ .8 = $200,000.

55.   **c.** Appurtenances are objects, rights, or interests that are incidental to the land and go with or pertain to the land, and constitute one of the three broad categories of real property.

56.   **c.** Spot zoning refers to the zoning of isolated properties for use different from the uses specified by existing zoning laws.

57.   **a.** The principle of substitution holds that buyers are generally unwilling to pay more for a property than for a substitute property in the area.

58. **b.** PMI *insurers the lender*, not the borrower, and covers the top amount of the loan in case of default.

59. **b.** Stating only the APR in an advertisement does not trigger the requirement for additional financial term disclosures.

60. **c.** A stigmatized property is a property having a condition that certain persons may find materially negative in a way that does not relate to the property's actual physical condition.

61. **c.** Susan's listing agreement with John was an exclusive agency listing. Therefore, if the house was sold within the term of the listing by anyone other than John, then John would owe Susan the full agreed-up on commission.

62. **a.** Although to be valid, a deed must be signed by the grantor, it need not be signed by the grantee.

63. **b.** *Jones v. Mayer* upheld the Civil Rights Act of 1866, using the Thirteenth Amendment as its legal basis.

64. **a.** Under the ECOA, a lender may ask if the applicant is married, unmarried (meaning single, divorced, or widowed), or separated, but may not ask if the applicant is divorced or widowed.

65. **b.** $300,600 = \$500 \times 601.2$. Therefore, because the transfer fee is $.75 for each $500 *or fraction thereof*, the transfer fee $= 602 \times \$.75 = \$451.50$.

66. **b.** In general, states with ample supplies of water have adopted water rights based on riparian rights.

67. **d.** A floodplain is an area of low, flat, periodically flooded land near streams or rivers.

68. **d.** Loss in value due to natural causes such as water damage or termites is referred to as physical obsolescence.

69. **c.** One of the disadvantages of an FHA-insured loan is upfront mortgage insurance premiums (upfront MIP) and annual MIP premiums.

70. **c.** Some states permit a broker to act *not* as an agent who represents one or more parties to a real estate transaction, but to act as a mere middleman who brings the parties together and lets the parties do all of the negotiating among themselves. Such a nonagent broker (also referred to as a *transactional broker, facilitator, intermediary, coordinator,* or *contract broker*) does not owe fiduciary duties to either party and is therefore not held to the same legal standards of conduct as is an agent. However, the states that permit this kind of nonagent status impose an obligation on the nonagent to act fairly, honestly, and competently to find qualified buyers or suitable properties.

71. **d.** An exclusive agency listing provides less security for the listing agent than does an exclusive right to sell listing because it allows the seller to procure a buyer without paying any commission to the agent.

72. **d.** George and Emily have no contract because a counteroffer is a rejection of the prior offer, and they have not agreed on a price.

73. **c.** The Civil Rights Act of 1866 prohibits racial discrimination in the lease or sale of all real property, commercial or residential.

74. **b.** Concealment refers to the act of preventing disclosure of something.

75. **c.** The comparable has a pool and landscaping combined value of $500 less than the subject pool and landscaping value. Therefore, the comparable value should be adjusted up by $500.

76. **c.** A plat is a detailed map showing the boundaries of the individual parcels, streets, easements, engineering data, and, often, the environmental impact of the development.

77. **a.** Joe has a dominant tenement because his easement is an easement appurtenant which can only exist if there is a dominant tenement.

78. **a.** Under the Superfund Law, a person may be able to assert the innocent landowner defense if before acquiring the property, the person undertook appropriate inquiry to ensure that the property was not contaminated.

79. **c.** Examples of expenses that are not deducted to obtain net income include mortgage payments and taxes on income.

80. **c.** Car payments would be included in a calculation of the total monthly expenses, but not in PITI.

81. **c.** A real estate broker owes a special relationship of utmost care, honesty, trust, and loyalty known as a fiduciary relationship to the broker's clients.

82. **d.** Natural hazard areas include flood hazard areas, fire hazard areas, and earthquake zone areas.

83. **b.** An implied contract is a contract not expressed in words, but, through action or inaction, understood by the parties.

84. **d.** A lease-option gives the optionee the right but not the obligation to purchase. Note that both the lease-option and the lease-purchase are bilateral contracts because each contains a promise by the optionor to lease and by the optionee to make the lease payments.

85. **d.** A voidable contract is a contract that is enforceable at the option of one party but not at the option of the other, as when the consent of one party (the party who may elect to have the contract enforced) is obtained by fraud (not forgery, which would render the contract void), coercion, misrepresentation, or undue influence.

86. **c.** Property tax paid on a homeowner's personal residence is tax-deductible.

87. **d.** To calculate gross rent multipliers, we do not consider income from any source other than rents. Therefore, in this case
gross monthly rent multiplier = $935,000 \div $3,400 = 275.

88. **c.** If at the end of a life estate, the future interest reverts to the grantor, the residue of the estate is called a reversion.

89. **b.** Police power, which is the power of government to impose restrictions on private rights, including property rights, includes building codes, zoning codes, subdivision regulations, and property setbacks.

90. **d.** When the three appraisal approaches give different valuations, an appraiser will arrive at a final estimate by the use of reconciliation.

91. **c.** In an adjustable-rate mortgage, the fully indexed rate = index + margin.

92. **c.** When a principal intentionally, or by want of ordinary care, causes a third person to believe another to be his agent who is not actually employed by the principal, an ostensible agency is created.

93. **c.** Most states require a listing agent to disclose the agency relationship to the seller before the seller signs the listing agreement.

94.   **a.** Pursuant to the statute of limitations, a contract that originally was valid and fully enforceable may become unenforceable after the passage of a certain amount of time.

95.   **a.** An assignment does not typically relieve the assignor of liability under the contract, so that if the assignee fails to perform adequately, the assignor may be sued for damages.

96.   **b.** An antitrust conspiracy occurs when two or more persons agree to act (referred to as "group action") and the agreed-upon action has the effect of restraining trade.

97.   **b.** Maximum PITI ÷ $6,000 = .32.
Maximum PITI = $6,000 × .32 = $1,920.

98.   **c.** A bundle of rights is all of the legal rights and privileges that attaches to ownership of property, which may include the right to possess, use, enjoy, encumber, sell, and/or exclude from others.

99.   **b.** A variance refers to an exception that may be granted in cases where damage to the value of a property from the strict enforcement of zoning ordinances would far outweigh any benefit to be derived from enforcement. As a general rule, variances are given only for rather minor departures from zoning requirements, relating to such things as setbacks, building height, and parking.

100.   **b.** The secondary mortgage market is the market wherein mortgages are sold by primary mortgage lenders to investors, such as pension funds and insurance companies.

101.   **d.** Typically, real estate law does not require that a licensee who is acting *solely* as a principal in a real estate transaction must reveal his or her status as a licensee.

102.   **a.** An agency is coupled with an interest if the agent has a financial interest *in the subject of the agency* (as distinct from the compensation that may result for the agent from his or her performance as an agent), which has the legal effect of making the appointment of the agent irrevocable.

103.   **b.** An ironclad merger clause is a contract provision stating that no prior agreement or contemporaneous oral agreement will have any force or effect.

104.   **d.** A good-faith estimate (GFE) of closing costs must be provided by any mortgage lender for a loan under RESPA. The GFE itemizes all fees and costs related to closing and must be provided to a potential borrower within three days after submission of a mortgage loan application.

105.   **c.** To avoid price fixing, real estate agents should avoid discussing prices (commission rates or referral fees) or pricing strategy with a competitor. Exceptions to this rule include that a broker may offer a competing broker a referral fee and discuss the amount of that fee, and may discuss with a cooperating broker how to split a commission or referral fee when negotiating regarding a particular transaction. Competing brokers may also receive compensation from either of, or both, the buyer and the seller.

106.   **a.** A lien is an official charge against property as security for the payment of a debt or an obligation owed for services rendered.

107.   **d.** A CMA typically will include data on three types of properties: (1) similar properties that have recently sold, (2) similar properties currently on the market, and (3) similar properties that have been on the market but whose listings have expired.

108.   **a.** The receiver of real property by will is known as a devisee.

109.   **c.** All states have enacted statutes that require brokers to inform parties to a real estate transaction as to whom the broker is representing.

110. **c.** In a special warranty deed, the grantors warrant that they own the property and have the right to convey it, and that the property was not encumbered during the period of their ownership.

Made in the USA
Lexington, KY
10 November 2015